Library Association Local Studies Group

Local Studies Libraries

Library Association guidelines for local studies provision in public libraries

...ries

SECOND EDITION

Working Group:
Patrick Baird, Martin Hayes, Alice Lock, Don Martin (Editor),
Ian Maxted, Aubrey Stevenson

LIBRARY ASSOCIATION PUBLISHING
LONDON

Published by
Library Association Publishing
7 Ridgmount Street
London WC1E 7AE

Library Association Publishing is wholly owned by The Library Association.

First published 1990
This second edition 2002

British Library Cataloguing in Publication Data
A catalogue record for this book is available from the British Library.

ISBN 1-85604-277-4

Also available from Library Association Publishing
Local studies librarianship: a world bibliography
Compiled by Diana Dixon for the Library Association Local Studies Group
ISBN 1-85604-307-X

Typeset in 13/15pt Garamond and Humanist 521 by Library Association Publishing.
Printed and made in Great Britain by MFP Design and Print, Manchester.

Contents

Introduction   vii

Main recommendations   ix

PART A: THE SERVICE

A1   The local studies service   1
A1.1   Definition   1
A1.2   The dynamic of local studies   1
A1.3   Aims and objectives   1
A1.4   Standards and targets   2
    A1.4.1   Annual Library Plans   3
    A1.4.2   Benchmarking   3
    A1.4.3   Quality of service   3
A1.5   Lifelong learning   4
A1.6   ICT   4
A1.7   Funding   5
    A1.7.1   Grant aid   5

A2   The user   6
A2.1   General principles   6
    A2.1.1   Social inclusion   6
A2.2   Customer interface   7
A2.3   Customer groups   7
    A2.3.1   Lecturers and students   8
    A2.3.2   Teachers and schoolchildren   8
    A2.3.3   Local historians   8
    A2.3.4   Family historians   9
    A2.3.5   Social/economic historians   9
    A2.3.6   Transport historians   9
    A2.3.7   Folklorists   9
    A2.3.8   Geographers/geologists   9
    A2.3.9   Archaeologists   10
    A2.3.10   Ethnic groups   10
    A2.3.11   People with disabilities   10
    A2.3.12   Commercial interests   10
    A2.3.13   Tourists   11
    A2.3.14   General library users   11
    A2.3.15   Future users   11

A3 Relationships 12

A3.1 Archivists 12

A3.2 Museum staff 12

A3.3 Film and sound archive staff 13

A3.4 Education staff 13

A3.5 Other library specialists 13

    A3.5.1 Other local studies librarians 14

    A3.5.2 Branch library staff 14

A3.6 Other local authority departments 15

A3.7 Media contacts 15

A3.8 Local history groups 15

A3.9 Other community groups 16

A4 Marketing and promotion 17

A4.1 Community awareness 17

A4.2 Minority ethnic groups 18

A4.3 Promotion 18

    A4.3.1 Talks 19

    A4.3.2 Exhibitions 19

    A4.3.3 Local history events 20

    A4.3.4 Publications 20

    A4.3.5 Press releases 20

    A4.3.6 Media interviews 21

    A4.3.7 Internet 21

    A4.3.8 Other outreach activities 21

A4.4 Marketing 22

A4.5 Local studies centres 22

PART B: RESOURCES   24

B5   The collection   24

    B5.1   Stock/collection policy   24
        B5.1.1   Bookstock   25
        B5.1.2   Newspapers and periodicals   27
        B5.1.3   Ephemera   28
        B5.1.4   Maps and plans   28
        B5.1.5   Illustrations   29
        B5.1.6   Recordings   32
        B5.1.7   Virtual resources   33
        B5.1.8   Archives   33

B6   Collection management   35

    B6.1   Conservation   35
        B6.1.1   Security   35
        B6.1.2   Storage/environment   35
        B6.1.3   Conditions of use   36
        B6.1.4   Repairs   36
        B6.1.5   Microform substitution   36
        B6.1.6   Negatives   37
        B6.1.7   Historical maps   37
        B6.1.8   Disaster plans   37
    B6.2   Stock management   38
        B6.2.1   Branch collections   38
        B6.2.2   Donations   38
        B6.2.3   Duplicate material   39
    B6.3   Classification and cataloguing   40
        B6.3.1   Digitizing the catalogue   41
    B6.4   Digitizing the collection   41
        B6.4.1   Networking   43
        B6.4.2   Metadata   44
    B6.5   Income generation   45
    B6.6   Publishing   46
        B6.6.1   Staffing requirements   46
        B6.6.2   Bibliographical standards   46
        B6.6.3   Authors   47
        B6.6.4   Pricing   47
        B6.6.5   Electronic publishing   47
        B6.6.6   Postcard publishing   47
        B6.6.7   Educational publishing   47
    B6.7   Intellectual property   48
        B6.7.1   Copyright   48
        B6.7.2   Right of access   48

B7   Staff   49

B7.1 The local studies librarian   49
B7.2 Supporting staff   50
B7.3 Training   50
B7.4 Volunteers and friends groups   51

B8   Facilities management   53

B8.1 Accommodation   53
    B8.1.1   Public study areas   53
    B8.1.2   Storage areas   53
    B8.1.3   Office accommodation   54
    B8.1.4   Open access provision   54
B8.2 Equipment   55
    B8.2.1   Storage equipment   55
    B8.2.2   Microform readers   55
    B8.2.3   Photocopiers   56
    B8.2.4   Photographic equipment   56
    B8.2.5   Sound and video recorders   57
    B8.2.6   Computers   57

Index   67

Introduction

Local studies librarianship has changed dramatically in the last 20 years, and the pace of change shows little sign of slackening. Local studies libraries play an increasingly acknowledged role in delivering the government's social and educational agenda, as well as recognizing, celebrating and recording local cultural and economic diversity. Local studies librarianship also forms an important plank in local community regeneration. There is also a wider recognition of the role of local studies libraries across the country in collecting and conserving the national published archive.

The numbers of researchers using local studies collections has increased significantly. So has the diversity of their backgrounds, the range of topics in which they are interested, and the economic activities in which they are engaged. In the past, local studies collections catered for those with traditional historical interests, which tended to be confined to the deeds of the rich and powerful in the distant past. Nowadays, research interests are concerned mostly with the lives of ordinary people in the local environment, past and present.

To meet this change in demand for services, local studies libraries have had to transform their collections strategies, the range of materials they provide, the ways in which they cater for and give access to the public – indeed, their perceptions of who their users are. Widespread computerization has facilitated the linking of materials in holdings of all types, from the current records held by local authority services, to the historic, including those in archives and museums. In addition, government emphasis on social inclusion obliges library services to reach out into communities that are not good users of libraries, as well as catering for long-established users. This may involve changes in collection strategy, the collection of materials in non-traditional media, changes in conservation strategy, and strategies to involve communities that have no traditional connections with library services. It is increasingly important to market and promote the service to all users: established, new and potential.

Change has been so rapid that research carried out in 1986 for the first edition of *Local studies libraries: Library Association guidelines for local studies provision in public libraries* was out of date before it was published in 1990. Subsequent attempts at revision were also overtaken by events. The new *Guidelines* that follow this introduction take into account these changes and take forward the 'New Library' vision of the late 1990s. The revolution in approach to the provision of all library services is reflected in these *Guidelines*. There is a broad-based commitment to ICT, extending out to, and linking up with local government information and services, emphasis on lifelong learning and the National Grid for Learning, as well as a commitment to social inclusion in the broadest sense. The *Guidelines* demonstrate the importance of local studies libraries in helping to deliver the government's social agenda, as well as showing how best to meet their obligations to local communities. To reflect this continuing change it is important that these *Guidelines* are not regarded as static but subject to constant reassessment and revision.

In recent years the position of public libraries in public life has been strengthened and redefined. The public library service is statutory, subject to some variations in detail in different parts of the UK, but until recently, there was no precise definition of statutory obligation. The relevant legislation, the Public Libraries and Museums Act of 1964, specified only that library authorities should 'provide a comprehensive and efficient service for all persons desiring to make use thereof'. Early in 2001, however, the Department of Culture, Media and Sport (DCMS) for the first time published public library standards, reminding local authorities in England of their obligations to meet certain minimum levels of service, and warning that failure to do so would invite government intervention. While the administrative context in other parts of the UK differs, the same commitment to standards is also present there. Future priorities for public libraries are set out in *New Library: the people's network*, published by the former Library and Information Commission in 1997. In the vision of this innovative policy document, local studies librarians play an important new role, as creators and providers of access to digital content from all over the UK.

Within the public library context, local studies is best considered in association with reference and information services. This edition of the local studies *Guidelines* should therefore be used in conjunction with the Library Association Information Services Group's *Guidelines for reference and information services in public libraries*, published in 1999. The *Guidelines* are intended as a toolkit for managers responsible for the appropriate services. Variations in population size and geographical area will, of course, mean that not all the recommendations are equally applicable to all authorities.

There is also a considerable overlap with the work of museums and archives, so it is essential that local studies librarians acquire a knowledge of present-day archive and museum practice. This reflects the view of government, which has placed the three sectors together in Resource but is not new to local studies librarians who have nurtured links with these two professions over many years. In fact, 'managing change' is not a new concept for local studies librarians and it is hoped that these guidelines will continue to support practitioners who have to carry the service into the new millennium.

Main recommendations

A THE SERVICE

AI The local studies service

The local studies service should:
- Set a full range of aims and objectives (A1.3)
- Set standards and targets, following the policies and guidelines laid down for the library service as a whole (A1.4)
- Feature in Annual Library Plans each year (A1.4.1)
- Take part in benchmarking exercises, using qualitative as well as quantitative indicators (A1.4.2)
- Play a full role in education and lifelong learning in all sections of the community (A1.5)
- Be seen as part of the core service in the library service's ICT strategies (A1.6)
- Monitor, on a regular basis, the level of funding needed to maintain the service, including the opportunities offered by lottery and other external funding sources (A1.7)

A2 The user

The local studies librarian should:
- Develop the library's vital role in promoting community awareness, local distinctiveness and social inclusion for all sections of society (A2.1, A2.2)
- Assist users by providing the resources for research and giving guidance in use of the material (A2.2)
- Provide equal levels of service to the full range of customer groups. These include lecturers and students, teachers and schoolchildren, local and family historians, social and economic historians, geographers and archaeologists, commerce, tourists and the media
- Address the requirements of ethnic groups and people with disabilities

A3 Relationships

Local studies staff should be prepared to work closely with:
- Other professionals in the heritage and education sectors including archivists, museum staff, sound and film archives, and education staff (A3.1, A3.2, A3.3, A3.4)
- Other library specialists (A3.5)
- Other local authority departments (A3.6)
- Local history and other community groups (A3.8, A3.9)

A4 Marketing and promotion

Local studies librarians should:
- Be aware of the potential of the local studies service to interact with local communities (A4.1)
- Realize the potential for meaningful work with ethnic minorities, especially when undertaken within their own communities (A4.2)
- Promote its services through a programme of talks, exhibitions and other events (A4.3.1, A4.3.2, A4.3.3)
- Publicize itself through newsletters and other library publications and appropriate media contact (A4.3.4, A4.3.5, A4.3.6)
- Maintain a dynamic presence on the internet (A4.3.7)
- Monitor its effectiveness through market surveys and statistics of use (A4.4)
- Be aware of the arguments for collaborating with museum curators and archivists to develop local studies centres (A4.5)

B RESOURCES

B5 The collection

The local studies service should:
- Formulate a collection policy for local studies material to ensure comprehensive coverage within the geographical area (B5.1)
- Ensure that adequate contingency funding is available to purchase items of local interest that appear on the market from time to time (B5.1)
- Have a flexible and wide-ranging approach to collection building (B5.1.1)
- Ensure that lending collections containing selected material of local interest are maintained (B5.1.1)
- Participate in national conservation and access projects, such as Newsplan (B5.1.2)

Local studies resources should include:
- A full range of monograph material, including items of current significance (B5.1.1)
- Locally published periodicals, newspapers (in original and microfilm), articles and cuttings files (B5.1.2)
- Local ephemera and grey literature, collected in co-operation with local museums and archives (B5.1.3)
- Historical and current mapping of the local area at all scales in hard copy and digital format (B5.1.4)
- Illustrations in all formats with access to photographic and digitizing facilities (B5.1.5)
- Sound and moving image recordings of local significance in co-operation with sound and film archives (B5.1.6)
- Local information in digital format (B5.1.7)

B6   Collection management

The local studies service should:
- Provide a policy for conservation of items in its collections (B6.1)
- Ensure adequate security of local studies stock (B6.1.1)
- Be familiar with currently recognized standards of storage and ensure that materials are stored in adequate environmental conditions (B6.1.2)
- Have access to specialist conservation facilities. (B6.1.3)
- Acquire microform or other surrogate copies to protect fragile originals (B6.1.5)
- Be covered by a library disaster plan (B6.1.8)

Local studies staff should:
- Maintain local studies collections in branch or community libraries (B6.2.1)
- Have a policy to encourage appropriate donations (B6.2.2)
- Draw up well-considered guidelines for the disposal of surplus material (B6.2.3)
- Catalogue and index their collections using systems that reflect the special nature of the documents and the local studies collection's position in the national published archive (B6.3)
- Develop integrated collection management systems to serve as networked computerized catalogues of all materials in local studies collections (B6.3.1)

Local studies libraries should:
- Develop programmes for systematic digitization of local content in cross-platform formats for national networks (B6.4.1)
- Ensure that images and other material digitized for networks are supported by adequate metadata (B6.4.2)
- Exploit the potential of local studies resources to provide income that can be applied to develop the collections (B6.5)
- Develop a publishing programme to improve access to local studies information (B6.6)
- Be aware of copyright and other intellectual property rights (B6.7)

B7   Staff

Every public library authority should:
- Maintain a local studies department, headed by a professionally qualified local studies librarian (B7.1)
- Train all library staff to be aware of the range of services provided by the local studies service (B7.3)
- Benefit from the enthusiasm of volunteers, wherever possible (B7.4)

B8 Facilities management

Every library authority should provide:

- Suitably designed accommodation with adequate public study areas and equipment to facilitate the use of a wide range of local studies materials (B8.1, 8.2.1)
- Secure storage areas with equipment to maintain the correct environmental conditions for the different types of local studies resource (B8.1.2)
- Adequate office accommodation (B8.1.3)

A THE SERVICE

A1 The local studies service

The local studies service exists to enable members of local communities to define their identity in terms of their own particular situation - family, home, community, region. Collections are established, developed and maintained as a public service, in the public interest. The ethos of public service is paramount. The service should form an integral part of the local information network, providing a clearly signposted point of entry to a wide range of local resources. The collections should complement those of other local services, such as archives, museums and local government information.

A1.1 Definition

> The term 'local studies', as applied to library local studies collections, covers the local environment in all its physical aspects, including geology, palaeontology, climatology and natural history, and in terms of all human activity within that environment, past, present and future.

A1.2 The dynamic of local studies

> A well managed local studies service will provide a dynamic bridge between the library service and potential users of all kinds within the community.

For example, local studies exhibitions will often attract new people into the library, some of whom may join the lending service and become regular library users. Others will find a comfortable path into the world of lifelong learning by starting with a local history investigation to chart familiar territory. The links that all local studies librarians forge with local and family history groups, and with many other local clubs and societies, can be of great value to the library service as a whole.

A1.3 Aims and objectives

> A local studies service should set for itself a wide range of aims and objectives. It should endeavour to:

- Be freely available to all people, whether or not they live in the local area.
- Meet the needs of disadvantaged individuals and groups.
- Provide opportunities for informal learning for all groups in society, giving them the chance to learn more about their own communities, enabling

them to develop their research and analytical skills, and so giving them the confidence to move on to other areas of study if they so wish.

- Provide a permanent and safe home for a comprehensive range of local studies materials, stored in proper environmental conditions.
- Preserve the community's documentary record to promote understanding and awareness of its development, community identity and pride.
- Provide a welcoming environment and quiet study area for lifelong learners at all levels.
- Provide staff who are properly trained in service guidance.
- Be responsive to customer needs.
- Offer a basic research service.
- Maintain a proactive collecting policy.
- Maintain a comprehensive range of finding aids for materials in the collections.
- Promote the awareness, use and enjoyment of collections.

A1.4   Standards and targets

➤ In setting standards and targets the local studies service must follow the policies and guidelines laid down for the library service as a whole, especially with regard to evaluation, performance measurement and benchmarking. The requirements of the Best Value regime must be observed.

Statistics of a range of local studies services should be maintained. If sufficient guidance on the kind of local studies statistics required as performance indicators is not available, performance indicators for reference services should be applied to local studies. For example, the Scottish Library and Information Council toolkit for *Implementing Best Value in public library services* (1999) suggests appropriate statistics for reference, local history and information services, including annual number of enquiries per 1000 population, a detailed quarterly sample of enquiries, various statistics relating to access and use of electronic resources, and annual expenditure on reference resources added to stock per 1000 population. Annual statistics of events and promotions and reference services income per 1000 population are also suggested. It is good practice to keep detailed statistics relating to events and promotions, such as the number of exhibitions mounted each year, numbers of people attending local studies talks, number of outreach visits to schools, and so on.

The DCMS Standards, as outlined in *Comprehensive, efficient and modern public libraries* (2001), include 'Percentage of library users reporting success in gaining information as a result of a search or enquiry' (PLS13) and 'Percentage of library users rating the knowledge of staff as good or very good' (PLS14) – both to be based on the National PLUS standards (Public Library User Surveys). These statistics are particularly important to the local studies library, and an attempt should be made to obtain broken-down figures in each case. Unobtrusive testing can also be used to determine user satisfaction.

A1.4.1 Annual Library Plans

➤ The local studies service should feature in Annual Library Plans each year.

Since 1998 library authorities in England have been required to produce an Annual Library Plan. Guidance on preparation of such plans was updated in 2001, following the publication of the DCMS Standards, which are intended to complement the Annual Plans and provide a link between planning and performance. Annual Library Plans of between 70 and 100 pages must be submitted to the full Council meeting of local authorities as well as to the DCMS. Because local studies provision forms part of the public library core service it should feature prominently in Annual Library Plans. It should also feature in other strategic planning documents of local authorities, such as Local Cultural Plans and Educational Development Plans.

A1.4.2 Benchmarking

➤ The local studies service must take part in benchmarking exercises, although the problems of drawing direct comparison with services provided by other local authorities are perhaps greater than in other areas of library provision.

Given the wide range and variety of communities served, and the differing local traditions and practices in local studies service delivery, it is difficult to establish benchmarks that would be applicable to all local authorities. Nevertheless there are sources that can assist in some areas. For example, a Library and Information Commission report on *The legal deposit of local publications: a case study of Leicestershire, Leicester and Rutland*, (Harris, Feather and Evans, 2000), provides information on the number of local publications that can be expected to be produced in a given area, of a certain population. It therefore provides help with establishing a benchmark for local studies acquisitions each year.

A1.4.3 Quality of service

➤ It is recognized that qualitative as well as quantitative indicators should be applied to the local studies service, perhaps more extensively than to other branches of the library service.

LAMSAC statistics, compiled in the 1970s but still a useful guideline today, showed that the average local studies enquiry took 10.52 minutes to complete, more than in any other area of reference service. This reflects the quality of answer expected in the local studies department. The Convention of Scottish Local Authorities (COSLA) *Standards for public library service in Scotland* (1995) identified six qualitative indicators of local studies service:

- Every library service should aim to be comprehensive in collecting and providing local studies material.
- Local studies collections should be actively promoted and their use encouraged.
- The library service should collect, record and preserve all appropriate material relating to the life of the community which it serves.
- Active collaboration should be developed with other appropriate local organizations to maximize the use of local resources.
- There should be an appropriately qualified member of staff in this field.
- Priority should be given to the conservation of unique materials.

The COSLA *Standards* also recommended that library authorities make use of *Local studies libraries: Library Association guidelines for local studies provision in public libraries*. It is intended that the present edition will be used as a matrix against which local studies activity can be logged.

A1.5   Lifelong learning

➤ Local studies libraries should play a full role in lifelong learning.

Experienced local studies librarians are very familiar with the concept of 'lifelong learning'. For years they have accommodated the expectations of self-improvers working on a variety of local projects, sometimes in the guise of formalized further education, but driven more usually by sheer determination. Recent research has shown that local studies can provide an attractive introduction to lifelong learning, with practitioners later branching into other areas of study. Local studies librarians are now expected to digitize local materials for learning networks. The digitized resources will sometimes in future be consulted in the customized 'People's Network' learning centres now introduced to libraries all over the country. However, they will also be accessed at terminals set up in local studies libraries, where users will be able to consult them in conjunction with the wide variety of materials held there. The Library Association policy paper on *Libraries and lifelong learning* (2001) noted that libraries offer a 'hybrid' concept, with resources in print, media and digital formats, and space for individual and/or group study. Most local studies libraries meet this ideal.

A1.6   ICT

➤ The local studies service is part of the core service, and it essential that this is reflected in library ICT strategies.

The service should share in and benefit from all new library ICT initiatives. A high percentage of any local studies collection is unique to the holding library service, and the catalogue records held locally for such materials may be the only ones available. It is the records for these local studies materials that attract the greatest external interest and, therefore, greatest proportionate use when the library catalogues are made available on the internet. The uniqueness of local collection material also identifies it as a high priority for digitization. As was pointed out in the *New Library* report:

> In local history, above all, libraries house unique collections. Digital tech-
> nologies will allow such collections . . . to be converted into new formats.
> This will make these resources more widely available, and their availability
> in digital format will facilitate security and conservation of the original,
> often inherently valuable, documents.

This message was emphasized by the findings of the *Virtually new* report, pub-lished soon afterwards, which confirmed that many libraries had already iden-tified their local studies collections as a priority for digitization. *See also* Sections **A4.3.7**, **B6.3.1**, **B6.4** and **B6.4.1**.

A1.7 Funding

> ➤ Local studies librarians need to monitor, on a regular basis, the level of funding needed to maintain the service.

It must be remembered that local studies departments require special injec-tions of funding on a more regular basis than other areas of the library ser-vice, for the mounting of commemorative exhibitions, publishing of local materials, purchase of unique items of local interest and other such purposes.

A1.7.1 Grant aid

> ➤ Local studies librarians should be aware of the opportunities offered by lot-tery and other external funding sources.

The library authority must be aware of the time necessary to prepare bids for grant aid, and should be asked to provide technical and specialist support. Many special projects in digitization, conservation and other areas of collec-tion development are only made possible by the Heritage Lottery Fund, Wolfson Foundation and other such sources. Sums available are often signifi-cant but submissions require a clear statement of aims and objectives, as well as familiarity with technical standards and the ability to produce complex ten-der documents and business plans. Bids have no guarantee of success and should not be undertaken lightly. The special expertise required in their prepa-ration might require support from other departments of the local authority.

A2 The user

A2.1 General principles

➤ Local studies play a vital role in fostering community awareness and identity. By maintaining and broadening a shared interest in our common heritage, the local studies service can actively promote the principle of social inclusion for all sections of society.

Users of local studies libraries come from all areas of society, irrespective of class, colour, religion, ethnicity, age or disability. The local studies library should aim to serve the needs of all users with equal care and attention. As some users are less able to explain their needs and requirements to library staff, the local studies librarian must be prepared to spend time with them, helping them to derive full benefit from the resources of the library.

A2.1.1 Social inclusion

➤ To meet the above requirement, the local studies librarian needs to understand the principle of social inclusion.

Social inclusion is often just considered in terms of race, religion, age, disability, education and/or social background, but as shown in the DCMS policy document *Libraries for all: social inclusion in public libraries* (1999) the concept is much more complex. Local studies librarians must be able to grasp this complexity, through familiarity with appropriate literature.

Libraries for all notes that a perception that 'libraries are not for us' exists both in individual and community terms, especially among:

* People who are educationally disadvantaged.
* People who live in isolation from wider society.
* People who don't think libraries are relevant to their lives or needs.
* People with a lack of knowledge of facilities and services, and how to use them.

The Library and Information Commission document *Libraries: the essence of inclusion* (2000) describes ways in which libraries and library staff can make inclusion happen 'everywhere for everyone'. These include the need to:

* Own the values and promote the culture of inclusion: maximize opportunities for the individual; avoid stereotyping; value the individuality of your library

users.

- Actively engage with and know your community; reach out to hard-to-reach groups . . .

Local studies libraries have a tradition of reaching out to communities and to the various groups within them. This tradition must be maintained and further developed, in the interests of social inclusion. The local collection should reflect cultural diversity, in its widest sense. *See also* Sections **A4.1** and **A4.2**.

A2.2 Customer interface

➤ The task of the local studies librarian is to assist users by providing the resources for research, drawing attention to groups of material that might prove useful (both within and beyond the immediate collection), and providing some guidance in use of the material.

Users normally carry out their own research, but it is sometimes appropriate for library staff to undertake such work to a limited degree. Requests for moderate amounts of subject information should always be accommodated. Special consideration should be given to postal or e-mail enquirers who are unable to visit the library through distance or disability. Widespread access to fax and e-mail facilities has led to an increase in the volume of such enquiries. This has increased the pressure on local studies services, which are not always able to respond to rising demand by increasing staffing levels proportionately. For this reason it is essential to allocate time and resources for such purposes according to a carefully worked out formula. It is the duty of the local studies librarian to ensure that adequate guidelines, based on allowable time, geographical disadvantage and other considerations, are available to help staff to make decisions in the varied cases they are likely to encounter. **Members of the public should always be informed about the levels of service they can expect free of charge**. The Library Association *Guidelines for reference and information services in public libraries* (1999) suggests a realistic time limit of 10-15 minutes for each enquiry, but in local studies libraries the allowance is often more generous, although not normally more than half an hour.

A2.3 Customer groups

➤ It is essential for the local studies librarian to develop an understanding of the full range of users expecting service from the local studies library.

Recently, use of collections has expanded enormously. Local studies libraries now have to cater for users from a wide variety of fields - educational, civic and commercial - including tourist and publicity officers, media personnel, economic development officers, market researchers, planners, amenity groups, leisure officers, community education staff and many others. This is in addition to the more traditional type of local/family historian, schoolchildren tackling projects, and increasing numbers of unemployed and retired people who find the study of local history a worthwhile and fulfilling pursuit. There has also been an increase in the number of overseas and other long-range enquiries, thanks to the ready availability of fax and e-mail facilities.

Some local studies librarians find it useful to maintain an index of profiles of regular users of the local collection, either in hard-copy format or on a database (ensuring conformance to the Data Protection Act). If successfully achieved this can provide a helpful overview of the research community. It can facilitate contact between researchers working on related topics; it can help to identify appropriate speakers when they are sought by community groups; it can help with stock selection and allocation of resources by providing information about local research priorities; it can also facilitate customer consultation on the part of the library.

Some of the customer groups most frequently in evidence are detailed below.

A2.3.1 Lecturers and students

It is important for local studies librarians to appreciate and understand the full range of adult learning activity in their communities, including university and college courses (nowadays more likely to include elements of local studies), part-time academic courses, open/lifelong learning activity, and so on. Local patterns of self-education should not be forgotten. The requirements of Open University students should also be borne in mind.

A2.3.2 Teachers and schoolchildren

School students need special guidance in use of the range of materials in the local studies library, especially when they need to be familiar with the use of primary sources. To structure this guidance to the requirements of the curriculum it is essential to seek the advice of education staff. Approaches should be made before each teaching session for the purpose of discovering which topics are likely to feature during the session. With regard to the provision of resources for the use of teachers and pupils in school premises, co-ordination with schools library staff is vital, and should be subject to formal agreement.

A2.3.3 Local historians

It is important to remember that many of the individuals who commit themselves to serious study of aspects of local history have no formal academic training. Local studies librarians need to be able to offer such individuals (who typically include retired or unemployed people) special guidance in the use of resources, and sometimes even in research and analytical skills.

A2.3.4 Family historians

Family historians likewise often require special advice on 'how to get started'. A range of printed guidance notes and/or information sheets should be prepared and made freely available to assist with this task. Many local studies libraries offer courses or workshops to the same end. Referral skills are also important in this field, as researchers will be keen to follow up non-local branches of their family. Because of the upsurge of interest in this area of study it is essential that local studies librarians acquire knowledge of the practices and principles of genealogy and family history. It is also important to maintain liaison with local family history societies, where such exist.

A2.3.5 Social/economic historians

Many researchers studying local aspects of social and/or economic history will be interested in profiles of non-local activity in those fields, for purposes of comparison. Referral skills are therefore important, and local studies librarians should acquire knowledge of suitable sources of information, including special collections and archives.

A2.3.6 Transport historians

Local historians studying aspects of transport history will be interested in the wider networks of canals, railways, turnpike roads, etc. Knowledge of appropriate resources held by neighbouring libraries is therefore useful to the local studies librarian, to facilitate the referral process. National and regional resources on transport history often incorporate detailed information relating to local communities and their transport services, and a knowledge of the whereabouts of such resources is also useful to the referral process.

A2.3.7 Folklorists

Local areas often have distinctive traditions in the fields of folk music, folk-tale, folk-dance etc. It is helpful for the local studies librarian to acquire knowledge of such traditions and the resources relating to them, to facilitate advice to researchers. An understanding of local dialect is sometimes needed for full appreciation of local folk tradition.

A2.3.8 Geographers/geologists

A range of special resources is needed to provide a service to local geographers and/or geologists, including statistics, maps, geological memoirs, etc. For example, background information is often needed in connection with the preparation of geo-technical site profiles prior to property redevelopment. As some of the local resources are of a technical nature, in large libraries they are sometimes located in science and technology departments, and not in the local studies library. Knowledge of such alternative locations is clearly essential for the local studies librarian.

A2.3.9 Archaeologists

Copies of fully published archaeological reports relating to local sites should always be acquired for the local studies library. Sets of unpublished records are sometimes held, but more usually they are only held at the local museum or by the local authority archaeologist. Knowledge of the location of such records is useful to the local studies librarian. The Durham Record project has promoted their wide availability in north-east England, as an eminently suitable category of records for digitization alongside maps and photographs.

A2.3.10 Ethnic groups

The history and traditions of minority ethnic groups established in the community now form a significant strand of local history in many parts of the UK. Special effort is needed on the part of the local studies librarian to maintain a full record of such communities, as appropriate documentation is sometimes difficult to acquire. However, perseverance will ensure that this important aspect of local history is recorded for the benefit of future generations.

A2.3.11 People with disabilities

Local studies librarians should ensure that provision is made for disabled people interested in local history. Attempts should be made to take local resources **out of the library** to interested groups or individuals who find it difficult to visit. Provision of audio tapes for people with visual impairment, and involvement in talking newspaper/audio magazine projects are also important. Local studies librarians should also be prepared to organize sets of appropriate photographs and other local materials for use by reminiscence therapy groups.

A2.3.12 Commercial interests

Local studies librarians should cater for the needs of commercial interests, with regard to local information and resources. For example, a range of local statistics should be maintained to facilitate the preparation of community profiles for business plans, etc. Policy with regard to charging the business community for the various services should be subject to careful consideration. As in all other cases a basic service should be provided free of charge.

In the case of local radio, television and newspapers, mutually beneficial arrangements can sometimes be made, especially with regard to publicity for the local studies service. In a similar way, the opportunity should be taken to remind local business firms that the local studies library is always interested in acquiring copies of annual reports, commercial literature, catalogues of products and other such publications.

A2.3.13 Tourists

Tourists and other holiday visitors often visit local studies libraries for the purpose of obtaining local information. Knowledge of local museum and tourist information services is essential, for local studies staff to provide referral advice in such cases.

A2.3.14 General library users

General readers often have recourse to the local studies library for answers to occasional questions or solutions to problems, e.g., background information for planning applications, legal disputes, information about rights-of-way, local byelaws, local addresses, quiz questions and trivia. Local studies staff must be familiar with routines for answering the most frequent of these, on a 'quick reference' basis. It is helpful to provide a special 'quick reference' collection of most-used local studies books and other materials, perhaps in a special bay adjacent to the staff desk.

A2.3.15 Future users

Local studies collections are planned as a permanent resource – to be held for posterity, or at least for a very long time indeed. The interests of future users should be regarded as of equal importance to those of present patrons; their probable needs should not be jeopardized by considerations of present-day convenience. Conservation for the future is of vital importance and is dealt with in Section **B6.1**.

A3 Relationships

➤ Close contact with professionals and amateur enthusiasts involved in other areas of local studies service is essential to the proper functioning of the local studies library.

Relationships with archivists and museum curators are particularly important. The Resource (Council for Museums, Archives and Libraries) manifesto invests museums, archives and libraries with joint responsibility for playing a central role 'in sustaining and developing cultural, social, educational and economic well-being', including the recognition and promotion of 'physical and social inclusion and cultural diversity'. Partnership and co-operation are listed as a core value.

A3.1 Archivists

➤ Local studies librarians must be prepared to work closely with archivists.

Present-day local authority staffing structures frequently determine that local studies librarians and archivists work together in the same department or section, or in departments/sections in close proximity to each other. Whether or not such situations prevail, it is vital that local studies librarians and archivists form a close working relationship and develop a mutual understanding, based on respect for each other's profession. Priorities, attitudes and training in the library and archive professions are quite different, but researchers cannot be expected to appreciate this, and it is important that the joint service provided to members of the public appears seamless. Every opportunity should be taken for co-operation and joint working on matters such as specialized training sessions, community projects, publishing, service promotion and co-ordination of service policies. Hayes (1997) has described an example of good practice.

A3.2 Museum staff

➤ Local studies librarians must be prepared to work in co-ordination with museum staff.

Local studies librarians sometimes work in the same department/section as museum curators, although perhaps less frequently than they do with archivists. Whatever the situation, however, it is equally important that good working relationships are developed, based on mutual respect and an understanding of the role of each other's profession. Referral of researchers, between local studies libraries, archives and museums will be an everyday occurrence. Co-operation between the professions, in the provision of a local studies service, is particularly important in rural areas. It is helpful for local studies librarians to share in and harness the enthusiasm that often attaches to museums and associated local history groups.

A3.3 Film and sound archive staff

➤ Local studies librarians should develop a working relationship with the staff of film and sound archives.

The special problems associated with the storage, indexing and access to sound and moving image materials has resulted in the establishment of collections of such materials, staffed by specialists, in different parts of the UK. Library staff can work with these specialists to ensure that locally identified material is forwarded for appropriate treatment. In return the film and sound archive staff can assist with provision of copies in more convenient format.

A3.4 Education staff

➤ It is important that relationships are forged between local studies librarians and education staff involved in local studies work, at all levels.

Two-way communication is vital, so that local studies librarians can be informed of the range of resources required for each course and gain familiarity with modern methods of teaching, while education staff can learn to appreciate the full variety of resources and services available in the local studies library. Consultation on schemes to digitize local studies materials, for educational purposes, is vital. Copies of promotional materials, prepared by the local studies librarian, should always be sent to schools, colleges and the appropriate departments of universities. Good understanding can sometimes also result in the deposit of written research in the local studies library.

A3.5 Other library specialists

➤ Co-ordination between specialists is important in all public library services and should be regarded as a basic essential of good management, but the special appeal of local studies provides a particular range of opportunities for joint working.

Outreach librarians will appreciate the ability of the local studies librarian to provide appropriate materials for the staff of homes for the elderly to employ in reminiscence therapy, also training in their use.

Children's/young people's librarians will often wish to co-operate over matters such as visits of school classes to the library, provision of local history materials for outreach visits to schools, preparation of children's exhibitions and displays on local topics, and organization of local history projects, competitions and quizzes.

Music librarians may seek co-operation over project work with local choirs, bands, orchestras and folk musicians.

Bibliographic staff will help to co-ordinate stock management, including local studies lending collections.

Reference staff will co-operate on many different matters, including the referral of enquiries.

Special services librarians will provide special help in many fields, especially ICT-related.

Non-public library staff in all levels of education, including university, college and school libraries, and in commercial and industrial libraries, may have a variety of interests in common. Those in education will often share the responsibility for local publishing/publications, while those in commercial and industrial libraries can facilitate the acquisition of reports, catalogues and other literature produced by local firms.

A3.5.1   Other local studies librarians

➤ Local studies librarians should be aware that their counterparts all over the country are facing the same challenges as themselves.

Expertise can be pooled by joint participation in regional bibliographical and resource lists, schemes for the distribution of materials, and participation in courses and day-schools. Much of this is co-ordinated by the Library Association Local Studies Group and its regional branches.

A3.5.2   Branch library staff

➤ Branch and community libraries have a vital role to play in establishing a close working relationship between the library service and its users.

In the field of local studies a genuine rapport can be generated, with local residents playing an active part in the collecting of local materials; in due course these can be used in the preparation of exhibitions, displays and publications for the enjoyment of the local community. In these processes the staff of each community library has an important part to play, for it is only by gaining the trust of local residents that the system of gathering and disseminating local materials can be fully operational. It is essential, in this context, that the local studies librarian maintains a good working relationship with community library staff, and provides them with training in the skills of involving the local community in local studies activities. In larger authorities local studies co-ordinators are sometimes appointed to maintain the link between the central local studies service and branch libraries.

A3.6 Other local authority departments

➤ It is important that understanding is achieved between local studies librarians and a wide range of staff in other local authority departments and sections, for the mutual benefit of all.

Planners will often seek information from the local studies library. In return they can provide facilities for the copying of maps and plans and supply copies of planning information leaflets and other publications. Planning departments nowadays often employ ecological, environmental, archaeological and/or architectural specialists who will clearly require access to library local studies resources. In return they will deposit copies of reports they produce.

Legal officers will require to consult the back-file of council documents and superseded editions of Ordnance Survey maps. In return they will provide up-to-date copies of council byelaws and other official documents for public use.

Press and publicity officers will require photographs and historical information for promotional purposes. In return they can provide publicity for the local studies library.

Leisure officers will require a range of local information, for example in connection with submissions for lottery grants, or environmental improvements. In return they can provide copies of the reports they produce.

Tourist officers will expect a wide range of local information for purposes of promoting the local area. In exchange they can provide copies of publications, including ephemera, undertake to sell library publications in their premises, and publicize library events.

Registrars and cemetery staff can take part in joint initiatives with local studies librarians over courses for training in the use of registers and other such documents.

A3.7   Media contacts

➤ Good relations with the local media will provide invaluable publicity for the local studies library.

Broadcasters from TV channels and radio stations often seek material from the local studies library for use in documentary and other programmes. They should be asked to reciprocate by providing video or sound recordings of the programmes, for preservation in the local studies library.

Local newspaper staff, who need frequent recourse to the local studies library for local information, should be invited to take part in initiatives for ensuring the preservation of newspaper files, in the various formats now available. They should also be expected to promote local studies library exhibitions, projects and publications in a reasonably comprehensive way. Liaison should be maintained on arrangements for the permanent preservation of the files of photographs that accumulate at local newspaper offices.

A3.8   Local history groups

➤ The enthusiasm of local history groups should be harnessed wherever possible.

Such organizations normally operate at a more informal level than other parts of the heritage sector, but they have often been in existence for a longer period of time. Across the country they are responsible for talks, exhibitions, publications, surveys and the maintenance of their own collections. The local studies librarian should be prepared to advise on the organization of such collections and should seek deposit or donation of copies of rarer items to the local studies collection.

A3.9   Other community groups

➤ Local studies librarians must encourage and develop close links with community groups of all kinds.

Community awareness is essential to the fundamental task of creating a permanent record of local activity, for use in the library, and this can only be achieved by developing a range of contacts within local organizations. Through these contacts the local studies librarian can identify and meet the relevant needs of community groups. As well as providing information from library resources, wherever possible the offer of space for groups to display material in the library should be made, and library exhibitions, displays and talks provided at group premises, as appropriate.

A4 Marketing and promotion

A4.1 Community awareness

> ➤ Local studies librarians should be aware of the potential of the local studies service to interact with local communities and service some of their most fundamental needs.

This potential has long been recognized, but has been notoriously difficult to quantify and express in a meaningful way. During the 1990s, however, an attempt to do so was made by the University of Sheffield Department of Information Studies, as part of an evaluation of the social impact of library services in Newcastle upon Tyne and Somerset, using 'social audit' techniques, through the medium of focus groups.

During this exercise the social value of local studies was clearly established. For example, it was shown that:

- individuals with no previous experience of adult education found the study of local history in the local studies library a comfortable gateway to further study.
- the local studies library acted as a 'community of common interest', where people with common interests could meet and share knowledge, both with each other and with the local studies librarian, who played a key role.
- incomers to communities found the local studies library to be a place where they could readily gain knowledge of their new home area.
- retired and/or bereaved people found library-based local studies to be a meaningful way of filling gaps in their lives.

These findings were considered to prove that criticism of the alleged 'heritage turn' of some public libraries was mistaken, especially as involvement in local studies often had a practical value, supporting an interest in 'conservation, and a regeneration within that conservation' (Usherwood, 1999). It could be added that much of local studies collecting policy is firmly bedded in the present day, for only by systematically acquiring present-day documents as they are created can the historical materials of future generations be secured.

Local studies librarians have long appreciated the value of identifying key people in small communities and forging strong links with such individuals, often persuading them to act as 'agents in the community' for the purpose of maintaining a presence for the local studies library at village or locality level.

Using such techniques, Strathkelvin District Libraries during the 1980s established a policy of targeting one small community each year, to promote grass-roots interest in the local studies service, gather materials (perhaps mouldering in people's attics, cupboards and drawers), mount an exhibition, and prepare a community history. With the involvement of local people in this way, the exhibition-launch became a real community event, a gathering of friends, relatives and acquaintances, attended also by representatives of local organizations and presided over by a councillor or other key local personality. If ready in time, the history book was launched along with the exhibition; otherwise its publication provided another opportunity for a community event at a later date. Beginning in 1985, eleven local communities were targeted in this way, with the result that local collections for these areas are now much stronger than before, and the library service is in a better position to service community needs. The techniques employed included the identification of former residents of the communities now living elsewhere but known to have local materials in their possession, in the hope that they might be persuaded to return them to their relevant context (see *Local Studies Librarian*, **13** (2), Autumn 1994, 3).

A4.2 Minority ethnic groups

➤ Local studies librarians must exploit the potential for meaningful work with ethnic minorities, especially within their own communities.

Everything possible should be done to ensure that all appropriate cultures are represented in the local collection, including material in a range of languages. If migration is identified as an appropriate topic for collection-building and project work, this will ensure that vital links with the different home lands are represented in the local studies collection. In this area of local studies, above all, it is essential to recognize that the history of the very recent past is just as important as older history. A special training programme for staff working with minority ethnic groups should be developed.

A4.3 Promotion

➤ Service promotion is a vital part of the work of the local studies librarian.

Events that are organized to strengthen community awareness on the part of the local studies service also serve to promote the local collection, to the extent that the concepts of 'community awareness' and 'collection promotion' become inseparably linked. In order for the local studies library to realize its full potential as a vehicle for social inclusion, it is vital that its collections are properly promoted and local people made fully aware of the range of services available to them. However, promotion can be an extremely time-consuming activity and it is important to achieve proper balance between this activity and the 'bread and butter' work of developing collections and answering enquiries. For maximum efficiency a **promotion strategy** should be formulated, determining the appropriate levels of staff time to be spent on the different aspects of promotion. This should be reviewed from time to time, to take into account the constant evolution of priorities, demands and emphases, and in particular the ever-increasing pressures on the time of local studies staff, in a whole host of ways. For example, it might not always be possible to provide talks for *all* groups that request them; in such situations it might be necessary to draw up a prioritized list of group categories.

A4.3.1 Talks

> ➤ All local studies librarians should be aware of the need to deliver a range of talks about the service they provide.

If the library possesses a suitable lecture hall talks on local studies topics can be provided there, but most of the talks undertaken by the local studies librarian will be on an 'outreach' basis, in the premises or meeting rooms of requesting organizations. Indeed, in the interests of social inclusion it is essential that a proportion of talks are external, to meet the needs of people with disabilities, older people, school classes and other groups and individuals unable to come to the library. They will usually be illustrated by 35mm slides or other traditional audiovisual aids, although nowadays PowerPoint software is being employed by some libraries, along with appropriate equipment, to make use of digitized materials for presentations. Care should be taken to ensure that the **practical use** of local studies materials is central to the theme of talks provided for local organizations. Case studies involving special events, subjects, places or people, brought to life using resources, can be particularly effective. Audience numbers should be recorded, for statistical purposes and to monitor effectiveness.

A4.3.2 Exhibitions

> ➤ Exhibitions should be mounted on a regular basis, as an effective way of promoting the local studies service.

An annual programme of local studies exhibitions should be planned, covering both internal library events and external displays, some perhaps on a circulating basis. Desktop publishing techniques enable local studies librarians to prepare effective exhibitions and displays unassisted, but for high-profile events the services of a graphic designer should be employed, either in-house (if available) or commissioned commercially. Care must be taken to ensure that subject information provided within exhibitions is properly researched and checked for accuracy. The local studies service should have access to an adequate range of display boards, preferably on a dedicated basis. Irreplaceable materials should always be located in locked display cases (provided with UV filters to counter the detrimental effects of sunlight), although it should be remembered that display cases are very easily damaged in transit between libraries.

A4.3.3 Local history events

➤ Bringing together speakers, societies and organizations to promote local or family history in general, or on a particular theme, is a very effective use of resources and can attract large numbers of people and generate extensive media interest.

They are best organized and financed on a joint basis with the local record office, museum or an appropriate society, the staff and/or members of which often have expertise in particular field, and can in any case share the workload. They should focus on a particular and well defined purpose, such as the promotion of a new publication or the celebration of a major anniversary. Attendance at conferences/fairs organized by neighbouring libraries/organizations can provide useful ideas and inspiration.

Since 1988 an annual 'Local History Week' has been organized in Scotland, as a joint venture between the Scottish Library Association and the Scottish Branch of the Local Studies Group (LOCSCOT). Libraries across Scotland have involved themselves with their local communities, and a great variety of events has been organized and promoted. Each year LOCSCOT now publishes a full list of the events countrywide, so that a permanent record of Local History Week activity will be available. In recent years a biennial Local History Week, on the Scottish model, has also been held in Northern Ireland.

A4.3.4 Publications

➤ Library publications can serve to promote the local studies service, especially if full information on sources is given as part of the text, with special emphasis on the relevant resources of the local studies collection.

Regular newsletters are also an excellent method of publicizing the service. A good example is the *Tameside Local Studies Newsletter*, published two or three times per year since 1997. Newsletters can be distributed in the library, council offices and to local history groups, or by means of a mailing list.

A4.3.5 Press releases

➤ Press releases should be prepared for all promotional activities.

They are best drafted by the local authority's press and publicity department, based on information provided by the local studies librarian, who should also check the final draft before release. If press releases are written by the local studies librarian, care should be taken to employ a style appropriate to the purpose. Where necessary, photographs or library literature should be sent with the release. A good personal relationship should be developed with newspaper staff, to enable meaningful follow-up to the stark simplicity of press releases to be accomplished on a regular basis.

A4.3.6 Media interviews

➤ Local studies librarians can often establish a strong bond of mutual interest with journalists and broadcasters.

Petty (1994) has effectively demonstrated the usefulness of this. Local studies librarians should certainly anticipate approaches from local press, radio and television companies seeking interviews to support local news features and stories, and should take advantage of any available in-house training courses on how to cope with such situations, which can be very demanding. Fundamental points should be memorized, and an attempt made to steer the interviewer towards them.

A4.3.7 Internet

➤ The internet provides an excellent opportunity for local studies librarians to promote their services, not just locally but on a worldwide basis.

Use can be made both of local authority websites and the websites of external organizations that invite local libraries to provide information on their holdings. The local studies website can include guides to collections, catalogues and listings of important sections of the stock, images of key illustrations, maps and other documents, topic guidance for users such as family historians, local history groups and teachers, details of coming events and even an online newsletter. Editorial access by local studies staff is vital to enable the essential task of keeping information up-to-date. If the format of the website is kept simple, this task can be undertaken by a wider range of staff. Simplicity will also facilitate speed of loading and full accessibility to the site through a wide range of equipment and browsers, including means of access for people with visual impairment. The future of local studies services on the internet will include the development of techniques for interactive communication, such as electronic enquiry forms and online publications order forms.

A4.3.8 Other outreach activities

➤ Initiatives, such as the Birmingham 'History Van', that take the local studies service into the community at grass-roots level, are an effective means of publicizing the service in areas that might not otherwise be penetrated.

Participational events, such as competitions, quizzes and local history trails, can also attract individuals who might otherwise be unaware of local studies provision in their area.

A4.4   Marketing

➤ It is vital that local studies librarians take steps to identify, as clearly as possible, the nature of the demand that exists for the services of the local studies library, and to gear their activities to respond to that demand.

Melrose (1999) has shown that it is essential for local studies librarians to market their resources. Indeed, she has suggested that if they do not do so their traditional strengths will be usurped by other organizations keen to maximize their own service value in a competitive world.

To enable local studies librarians to market their services in an effective way they need good information about the level of demand for these services in the community. Statistical information can be obtained by means of conventional library service or local authority questionnaires, or by special local studies questionnaires, made available in the local studies library, or more importantly, at external events, such as talks, exhibitions, conferences and history fairs. Additionally, as mentioned previously, Usherwood (1999) has shown how 'social audit' techniques, through the medium of focus groups, can provide extremely valuable information about the aspirations of communities and individuals. Local societies and organizations, of all kinds, can also provide this kind of information through their regular links with the local studies library, while website 'hits', if properly analysed, can provide additional statistical evidence.

Once priorities have been identified, promotional activities can be targeted in a more effective manner. Hayes (1995) has demonstrated the value of a special events group to co-ordinate the promotion of events within a local authority service, involving library, archive, education, planning and public relations staff. Co-ordination between departments, in this way, is an effective means of marketing local authority services, as it enables the sharing of a wide range of experience and knowledge of the community and its true requirements.

A4.5   Local studies centres

➤ Local studies librarians should be aware of the advantages of collaborating with museum curators and archivists to develop local studies centres.

The practice of establishing 'local studies centres', embracing archives, museums and local studies libraries (or more frequently only archives and local studies), has been around for some time, notably in the London boroughs, but also in other cities and towns throughout the UK. In theory, location of the local studies library, the local museum and the archives department in close juxtaposition, with the staff of all three working in co-operation, is of the greatest convenience to users. Additionally, for the service as a whole, economies of scale mean that specialists such as conservators, graphic artists and education officers are more likely to be appointed, to the advantage of all three disciplines

In practice, there can be drawbacks to this approach. During times of financial pressure, local authorities are likely to consider local studies centres as legitimate targets for funding cuts. There may be reductions in staff, even to the extent that one of the professions (most likely the local studies librarian) is no longer represented. Also, for the idea to succeed, it requires the full co-operation of all three disciplines, and this cannot always be guaranteed. Reservations have been voiced by some archivists. Rimmer (1992, 1998), for example, has attacked the local studies centre concept. He argues instead for the 'professional and intellectual independence of the librarian, archivist and museums officer' and criticizes the policy of 'synergism' (i.e. the merging of units with similarities), this having been discredited, as a management approach, in the USA. However, with the establishment of Resource, it is clear that UK librarians, archivists and museum curators are expected to work together towards the achievement of common goals, so it seems possible that the local studies centre ideal will be given fresh impetus.

From a professional librarian's point of view, links between local studies and other divisions of the library service are of vital importance, and every attempt should be made to retain and strengthen them, whether local studies centres are established or not. If ideals of community awareness are to be promoted effectively, the dynamic operation of the local studies service through branch or community libraries is vital. The network of branches, and the opportunity it offers for meaningful community involvement, is unique to public libraries and should never be underestimated.

From the user's point of view, provision of an apparently seamless service is logical and therefore appreciated. All three professions should seek to work together to achieve this end.

B RESOURCES

B5 The collection

B5.1 Stock/collection policy

➤ Library authorities must formulate a collection policy for local studies material.

This should reflect the diversity of the community served. It should define:

- The topographical scope of the collection.
- The forms of material to be collected.

The collection policy needs to be reviewed at regular intervals.

It is becoming increasingly clear that local studies collections across the country have a vital role to play in maintaining the distributed national published archive. Surveys have shown that, even with the benefit of legal deposit, the British Library receives a lower proportion of local publications than many local collections. It is important, therefore, that collection policies, supported by adequate funding, enable local studies libraries to fulfil this role effectively.

Once the definitions have been agreed upon, comprehensiveness within their scope should be the aim. The policy should take into account the aspirations of other local repositories seeking similar material, especially museums and record offices, and full discussion should take place with the professional staff in charge of such repositories. In this way joint agreement can be reached, eliminating both competition and unnecessary duplication, and facilitating convenience of user access. Ability to provide the proper conditions for long-term conservation should always be of prime importance. If the local record office or museum can provide better conditions, this will often determine the best location for certain types of material.

Subject to the requirements of conservation, convenience of users is of great importance. Libraries are open for long hours, are often conveniently situated, are freely accessible to all, have catalogues and indexes that may be easily consulted, have good seating accommodation, and access to facilities such as photocopiers, microfilm/microfiche readers, and ICT equipment. Therefore, provided that the criteria for conservation can be met, the library is an ideal location for non-archival local studies material. Funding must be sufficient to provide an adequate range of books and other local studies resources. To this end it is desirable that local studies libraries have their own separate budget, of sufficient purchasing power.

Arrangements should also be made to ensure that adequate contingency funding is available to purchase items of local interest that appear on the market from time to time, bearing in mind that such opportunities can occur at any time of the financial year. A new local studies collection will require special funding during the early years of growth.

B5.1.1 Bookstock

➤ Local studies libraries should have a policy on levels of comprehensiveness.

Many libraries have traditionally adopted a policy of 'total comprehensiveness' with regard to the acquisition of local books and pamphlets, regardless of quality, bias, literacy or any other consideration. Others, particularly in large cities, have followed a more critical standard, rejecting items they have deemed unsuitable for library stock. In the era of desk-top publishing, when much greater numbers of local books and pamphlets are produced, including many of an obviously poor standard, there is perhaps a stronger argument for the critical approach. This should, however, involve careful examination of all items before deciding which to reject. It is also important to consider storage capacity and cataloguing workload.

➤ Local studies libraries must have a flexible and wide-ranging approach to collection building.

Once a book or pamphlet has been accepted as suitable for stock, multiple copies should be acquired in order to ensure adequate resources for present and future needs. Antiquarian booklists and shops should be actively searched in order to acquire out-of-print titles. A cash 'float' should be available, to facilitate instant purchase, where necessary, of items discovered in bookshops, at local and family history fairs, and elsewhere. Donations from members of the public should be sought, especially to fill gaps in the collection. Gift and exchange systems, both national and local, should be developed and encouraged to improve local studies collections. Individual direct offering of material between libraries should also be practised.

➤ Staff should be aware of new opportunities for searching electronically offered by digitized bibliographies.

These include the use of online services to identify periodical articles relating to local topics or events. Publishing societies of local or regional importance (e.g., record societies, parish register societies) should be supported by subscription or grants as generously as resources allow, for such societies are often significant publishers of local information, usually of a high standard. All library staff (throughout the service) should be trained to be alert to the identification of relevant locally published material.

➤ Acquisitions should include materials of current significance.

As well as historical material, relevant current publications of all kinds should be sought, including all local authority publications. Bodies that often produce important materials include social, political and cultural organizations, churches, schools and local industrial and commercial firms – the list will vary according to local circumstances. Most local authority publishing is unco-ordinated, and active pursuit of this material from its various sources is essential. Appropriate general reference tools, bibliographies, and guides to the methods used in local studies should also be available in collections.

➤ Acquisitions should include works by local authors.

In addition to collecting material about the locality, many local studies libraries collect works by authors associated with the area, regardless of subject matter. In some cases the influence of the author's local background on a creative work is fairly easy to determine, in others less so, while in many instances the link between the author and the locality can be extremely tenuous. Care should therefore be taken to establish criteria by which the works of local authors are acquired for comprehensive or selective representation. Creative works set in the local area, even those by non-local authors, should be acquired.

➤ Acquisitions should include locally printed items.

A number of local studies libraries hold special collections of locally printed material, perhaps including early printed works, private press books, hand-made books and other special categories. Where appropriate, the local studies librarian should report these for inclusion in national catalogues of specialized printing, such as the *English Short Title Catalogue* (ESTC).

➤ There should be co-operation between libraries in the acquisition of reprographic copies.

Some local studies libraries hold special collections with significance beyond the boundaries of the local area (e.g. collections of material relating to local authors of national reputation). The local studies librarian has a responsibility to publicize such material outside the local area. Digital or reprographic methods of copying should be used to provide items not obtainable in hard copy; such copies can also be used to save wear and tear on rare items. Adequate microform and/or ICT equipment should be provided for these purposes.

➤ Lending as well as reference collections should be maintained.

While it is inevitable that consultation of the main local studies collection will be on a 'reference only' basis, a complementary home reading collection will be appreciated by readers unwilling or unable to undertake all of their research on library premises (or who wish simply to take home a local book to read). A lending set of the most useful and popular local books, both current and out of print, should therefore be assembled as soon as the availability of duplicate material permits. This collection should be administered directly or indirectly by the local studies librarian to enable him/her to monitor the global stock of individual titles held within the library service and ensure that this does not fall below an acceptable level.

B5.1.2 Newspapers and periodicals

> Locally published newspapers, including free newspapers, are of prime importance and should be collected exhaustively and preserved on a permanent basis.

Responsibility for implementing local NEWSPLAN recommendations should be borne in mind. Local collecting policy will embrace newspapers held on microfilm/microfiche, and increasingly CD-ROM. The facility for free-text searching of newspapers on CD-ROM or other electronic formats might in future eliminate the need for conventional newspaper indexes. In the meantime, however, these still fulfil an extremely useful function in the local studies library, and will continue to be prepared. A useful guide, in this connection, is *Guidelines for indexing newspapers*, published by the Local History Panel of the Library and Information Service Council (Northern Ireland) in 1997.

> As the permanence of electronic formats cannot yet be guaranteed, hard copy and/or microfilm will continue to form the basis of newspaper preservation policy.

Microfilm produced by the British Library, and by the Scottish and Welsh Newspaper Microfilming Units, is of a high standard and will last for hundreds of years, perhaps longer than the original newspapers in some cases. Some libraries no longer bind original copies of local newspapers, storing them instead in archival boxes, a policy that is technically sound, from the point of view of conservation, provided that steps are taken to ensure that individual copies are not allowed to go missing from the file. Microfilm should never be seen as a complete substitute for original newspaper copies. A file of the latter should always be retained.

> Periodical publications relating to local studies must be collected.

In addition to newspapers, other local journals of all types should be collected, including journals and newsletters of local societies; parish, school and college magazines; house journals of local firms; commercial and industrial newsletters; and newsletters of bodies such as local parish or community councils.

Periodicals dealing with the techniques of local history and archaeology, also family history and genealogy, should be represented in the collection, e.g. periodicals such as *The Local Historian*, *Local History*, *Scottish Local History* and *Family Tree*. These can provide useful information for the local studies librarian on new or updated resources.

➤ Relevant articles should be identified in newspapers and periodicals, both local and national.

The collection should be supplemented by copies of relevant articles in periodicals and newspapers not otherwise added to library stock (copyright permitting). It is essential to alert staff working in other library departments so that they identify local material in the stock of these departments, and inform the local studies librarian of items identified.

➤ News cuttings are important in the local studies library, even when a complete run of a newspaper is held and indexed.

Cuttings provide ready dossiers of information for researchers, which can easily be browsed and photocopied, and can also provide a convenient source of material for exhibition purposes.

B5.1.3 Ephemera

➤ Local studies libraries should acquire a range of local ephemera.

Acquisitions policy should embrace ephemeral materials such as trade catalogues, programmes for local events, annual reports of local organizations, posters, timetables, sale catalogues, election publicity and other political material, catalogues of local exhibitions, and publicity material issued by local firms. Care should be taken to distinguish between ephemera and archival material (e.g. large collections of bills or receipts providing evidence for business history) that might be more appropriately located in a record office. Local studies librarians should be aware that collections of ephemera are often held by local museums. In such cases, there should be careful co-ordination of policy.

B5.1.4 Maps and plans

➤ Local studies libraries must provide access to a comprehensive range of historical and current mapping of the local area.

Ordnance Survey maps

Collections should include all maps published for the defined area at scales of 1:10,000 (6in. to 1 mile) and larger. For libraries with large rural coverage this will not always be possible in the short term, but a gradual and methodical programme to complete collections by acquisition of modern reprographic copies should be undertaken, subject to the restrictions of the copyright acts. As an alternative to hard copy, microfiche of the first and second editions of the County Series 1:2,500 is available from the British Library. Smaller scale Ordnance Survey maps should also be sufficiently represented in the collection to meet the needs of researchers. Discontinuance of the publication of 1:10,000 and larger scale maps, in favour of the production of individual map sheets to the customer's order, threatens the future of this important source of historical information in local studies libraries. Making full use of procedures permitted under local authority service level agreements, library staff should develop strategies to ensure that orders for appropriate map sheets are generated regularly, so that the continuity of collections is maintained. Unfortunately, there is no longer a guaranteed standard for such products. They employ a wide variety of software packages and result in map images where the data elements included may not correspond to those contained on the former published editions. Maintaining the continuity of the national large-scale map archive in a widely available standard format is a problem that will require a solution at national level.

The ready availability of earlier editions of Ordnance Survey Maps in high quality digital format will be vital to the future of local studies initiatives. Commercial considerations will probably continue to ensure that such digitized information will be costly, but local studies librarians will need to find solutions to the problems of access. Attention should be paid to the selection of the most suitable degree of resolution for different purposes, and to the 'binary' versus 'greyscale' argument (Parry, *Virtually new* report, 1998, pp. 29-30).

Other maps

Non-Ordnance Survey maps of all scales and dates, including geological, land-use, street maps, administrative/boundary maps and Experian Goad shopping centre plans, should be comprehensively collected. Archival maps, containing unique information, belong more properly in a record office, although copies can be made for the local studies library, where appropriate.

B5.1.5 Illustrations

> ➤ Local studies libraries should maintain and provide access to collections of local photographs and other illustrative material.

Photographs form an important part of library local studies collections, and are much in demand. Other institutions, especially museums and record offices, also collect photographs, and close co-operation between the relevant repositories to develop policies for acquisition, storage and public accessibility are highly desirable. Published postcards may or may not be integrated with other photographic collections, but the above principles apply.

➤ Local studies libraries should initiate programmes for the digitization of their illustrations collections.

Some libraries have now digitized many of the photographic images in their local studies collections, and indeed widespread programmes for the digitizing of photographs are ongoing. These can reduce the need for handling originals in the local studies library, can enable the images to be made more readily available at branch library level, and indeed, by means of the internet, can facilitate wide public access to the library's collections. However, local studies libraries will continue to handle original photographs and negatives as an important part of their work, and a knowledge of traditional practices and procedures will continue to be required for the foreseeable future.

➤ Negatives of all photographs should be acquired, for purposes of security.

Subject to the limits of copyright (which in the case of donated photographs should be clarified at time of acquisition), it is desirable that every photograph should be copied and a copy print made available for day-to-day use, with the negative filed separately from the print. Although this may not be achievable in the short term, especially with large collections, such a policy will provide insurance against damage and theft. Negatives should be acquired wherever possible, and always when a photograph is commissioned (i.e. negatives should not be filed at the photographer's studio). The black and white negative is still regarded as the most stable form of permanent photographic record and should form the main corpus of the collection. Original photographic prints should also be held as part of the permanent record, and care taken that appropriate storage facilities are provided for their conservation.

➤ Detailed descriptive records of photographs should be maintained.

Full details relating to a photograph should be recorded separately from the print on acquisition, including identification of the subject of the photograph, its date, donor or other source of acquisition, and whether copyright restrictions apply. If the negative number is added to the record, it can prove useful when prints are lost or damaged, and can also be used for indexing purposes. Whenever possible, modern technology should be employed to facilitate the protection of original photographs, and provide better indexing and easier access.

➤ Colour versions of photographic records should be acquired wherever possible.

Colour prints and slides are a useful supplement to photographic collections. Whilst a colour slide is less convenient than a print for library use, it is the most economical form of colour record and the quality is technically superior to that of a colour print. Moreover, a collection of colour slides is an important educational aid, and can be used to publicize the local studies library. Duplicates should be made for educational use, in order to prevent deterioration of originals. If lending of slides to individuals for the purpose of illustrating lectures or talks is undertaken, a database of customer profiles can provide guidance in customer requirements and responsible practice (*see* Section **A2.3** above).

➤ Local studies libraries should take part in local photographic surveys.

Library photographic collections should always include coverage of the present day scene. Towards this end local studies librarians should organize photographic surveys of local scenes and events. A pioneer scheme was begun in Chester in 1963, at the instigation of the local Civic Trust. The city's Reference Librarian became involved at an early stage and agreed to arrange for the cataloguing and filing of the results of the photographic surveys in the library. The main record was in the form of 35mm black and white diapositive slides; negatives and contact prints, the latter as part of a visual index to the collection, were also prepared. The Chester Survey has continued ever since, more recently with the addition of 35mm colour slides to the black and white record. An awareness of local redevelopment schemes is essential in order to enable 'rescue' photography to be undertaken effectively. Whilst much record work will be carried out by the library or a paid agent, local photographic societies sometimes offer willing help; provided assurances are sought that processing is to a satisfactory standard, such links should be welcomed both on financial and community grounds.

Sometimes photographic surveys carried out by other Council departments, in connection with archaeological or architectural care, environmental development, planning, building control, etc., can be acquired by the local studies library for permanent preservation. Aerial photographs should be purchased as extensively as funds allow. Although expensive, they are vital to some areas of historical research.

➤ Access to an in-house photographic department is desirable.

Ideally, the library should establish its own photographic department with professional staff, equipment and darkroom facilities. An in-house department of this kind can be of great benefit in ensuring security of items loaned for copying, in facilitating the making of copies for display purposes and for sale, and in implementing a planned programme of record work such as that outlined above.

➤ Digital copies of photographs should be made available to library users wherever possible.

Increasingly, library users expect inexpensive digital copies of photographs to be available for purchase, as an alternative to conventional photographic prints from negatives. It is a great advantage if equipment for the preparation of such digital copies can be readily available. It should always be remembered that the permanence of colour copies is likely to be poor.

Drawings, watercolours and prints and engravings are sometimes routinely directed to a local museum or art gallery, although many local studies libraries maintain collections of such items. It is essential that a common policy is agreed with appropriate museums and galleries. Sometimes topographical subjects are held by the library and other works of art by the museum or gallery; or perhaps unframed items are accommodated by the library and framed items by the museum/gallery. Where drawings, watercolours or prints are held by local studies libraries, advice concerning their conservation should be sought from museum/art gallery staff. Consideration should be given to acquiring 35mm slides or other copies of relevant works of art held in other repositories.

B5.1.6 Recordings

➤ Local studies libraries should maintain collections of sound and moving image recordings of local significance.

Public use of all recordings, whether sound or visual, should always be from a copy and not from the original. If local sound or film archives are available, originals can be deposited there for safekeeping, the library having copies made for its own use. Libraries should take every opportunity to co-operate with specialist organizations, such as sound and film archives, that are a valuable source of expertise and can often provide specialized services.

Detailed cataloguing of recordings, describing their contents in full, is essential, as their physical format precludes adequate reference access in any other way.

Sound recordings

Sound recordings representing the social background and occupation of the community often form a valuable part of local studies library stock. Such recordings are particularly important when the sound is of interest in itself; for instance, dialect, folksong. Other recordings that can be especially useful are those giving details of working practices in local trades and industries, and those describing the outlook, lifestyle and social background of the interviewees. Such recordings often serve to fill significant gaps in printed sources. Arrangements with local radio stations can sometimes be made for deposit of local material used for broadcasting.

In addition to sound recordings of the kind described above, commercially produced tapes and discs (e.g. of local choirs) should be acquired. Talking newspapers for the blind are now produced in many districts and should be acquired, perhaps selectively, for local studies collections.

Visual recordings: film

Cine film has the advantage of permanence and is still the most desirable medium for conserving visual moving images. **Warning:** There is a serious danger of spontaneous combustion occurring in cine film made before 1951. If any such film is held, professional advice concerning its treatment and/or disposal should be sought **as a matter of urgency**.

Visual recordings: video

Although a medium rapidly expanding in use, videotape is not of reliable permanence. Video recordings will often form part of the stock of a local studies collection, but in cases where material merits long-term preservation, professional advice should be sought with a view to preparing master tapes in digital format. Rare material on film can be transferred on to video, CD-ROM or DVD to increase its availability.

B5.1.7 Virtual resources

➤ Local studies librarians should be aware of the potential value of local information available in digital format.

Much local information exists in digital format only, sometimes on CD-ROM or other disk format, but often only on computer networks and therefore subject to removal and permanent loss. The websites of local football and other sports clubs are common examples. Local studies libraries should find ways of archiving significant information from local websites, perhaps in a selective way, to reflect the changing scene. Printouts can be made for the purpose, but the appropriate local organizations should always be approached for permission to re-format their information in this way.

B5.1.8 Archives

Authorities with a responsibility for archives should recognize that this implies a commitment to staff and accommodation, so that fully professional standards for archival storage, access and conservation can be achieved.

If this commitment cannot be met, archive material should be transferred to the most appropriate repository able to provide full archival care. As an ideal, local archives and library local studies collections should be housed in close proximity, for the convenience of researchers (*see* Section **A4.5**).

B6 Collection management

B6.1 Conservation

➤ Local studies libraries must have a policy for conservation of items in their collection.

The local studies collection usually contains a high proportion of material that is rare or unique (and often fragile). It is the duty of the local studies librarian to give high priority to protecting such resources from theft, and from damage by unfavourable environments. Proper environmental control will help to reduce the need for expensive conservation work in course of time. Useful information can be obtained from the National Preservation Office. The NPO website includes a list of publications, some of which are available free of charge, and answers to some 'frequently asked questions' on preservation (**www.bl.uk/services/preservation**).

B6.1.1 Security

➤ Security of stock in the local studies library is vital.

To this end there should be constant vigilance by staff at all times. Users should be registered, with application forms completed for closed-access stock, and proof of identity provided before issue of rarer items. Bundles of documents can be counted or weighed using finely calibrated scales, before and after use. If space and staffing resources allow, a bag-store should be provided at the library entrance, to reduce the risk of items being stolen. Although costly, security tagging is an excellent means of protecting books against theft. In the local studies library some items may be unsuitable for tagging because of their fragile nature.

If items are removed from the local studies library for photographic copying, binding, exhibition, or other such purposes, the local studies librarian must take appropriate steps to ensure the security of such items when outside his/her custody.

B6.1.2 Storage/environment.

➤ Local studies librarians should be familiar with currently recognized standards of storage.

Such standards cover matters such as temperature, humidity and appropriate stationery for all materials in their care, whether these are books, documents, recordings or other types of resource. They should be familiar with the British Standard Recommendation for *Storage and exhibition of archival documents* (BS5454). Care should be taken to protect books on library shelves from sunlight or other adverse conditions. Staff should be aware of guidelines and policy statements that have been issued by The Library Association and other relevant bodies (*see* Bibliography).

B6.1.3 Conditions of use

➤ The issue of old and/or fragile material should be governed by a set of carefully drawn-up 'conditions of use'.

Pencils only should be used for note taking, and researchers should be advised not to lean on documents or lick fingers to turn pages. Archival polyester sheets can be placed over documents to prevent marking or creasing. The photocopying of fragile originals should not be permitted whatever the circumstances (and, indeed, some libraries have even considered it necessary to discontinue public photocopying facilities in the local studies department altogether because of the high incidence of damage to such items).

B6.1.4 Repairs

➤ All local studies librarians must have access to conservation facilities for the repair of books, maps and documents.

If internal conservation facilities are not available, the advice of a local record office should be sought and use be made of the facilities there, if possible. Otherwise, an outside firm of conservators should be employed; a fully professional conservation service is provided by some of the binderies that specialize in library work.

B6.1.5 Microform substitution

➤ To prevent undue wear and tear, it is often necessary to use a microform or other copy instead of the original.

This is desirable with rare items, and when the original form is particularly vulnerable to deterioration (e.g. newsprint). When a copy is made for this reason, it must be used instead of the original (except in very special circumstances). Microfilm negatives should be stored in secure microfilm cabinets away from both the positive film and the original copies.

B6.1.6 Negatives

➤ Photographic negatives should be stored separately from prints, preferably at a separate site, as a precaution against total loss in the event of mishap.

B6.1.7 Historical maps

➤ Reprographic copies of historic maps should be made for everyday use to facilitate conservation of originals.

Where digital versions are made, these can serve the same purpose. With intensive public use maps can deteriorate very rapidly.

B6.1.8 Disaster plans

➤ It is essential that local studies collections enjoy the protection of a disaster plan.

The local studies librarian should be aware of the necessity for a library disaster plan, and if none exists should convince senior staff of the need for one. When library disaster plans are being prepared, the local studies librarian should provide significant input.

Very often a high proportion of the irreplaceable material in a library's stock is located in the local studies department, as proved to be the case when Norwich Central Library burned down in August 1994. The Norwich fire provided significant lessons in disaster planning, particularly with regard to the care and maintenance of electrical wiring. The disaster report recommended the installation of sprinkler systems, and fire-resistant doors and screens, where possible.

It should be realized that disasters vary greatly in magnitude and can include crashes of IT systems as well as damage caused by fire, flood or explosion. For larger disasters agreements for co-operation with record offices, museums, cold stores and others need to be in place, and lists of emergency contacts should be updated on a regular basis. Ideally, neighbourhood disaster plans should be available for heritage collections, as the local studies library may be required to assist in disaster relief for incidents that occur elsewhere, for example by supplying temporary storage or operating an emergency enquiry service. Risk analysis should identify a range of strategies for coping with different scenarios and should include an assessment of the local studies collection to prioritize categories of stock for salvage. Irreplaceable material should be identified and a realistic valuation prepared, to cover the cost of replacing as much of the information content as possible. Guidance is available from sources such as the National Preservation Office, the Blue Shield scheme and the M25 Consortium Disaster Control Planning Site on the internet (**www.m25lib.ac.uk/M25dcp/**). Commercial services such as Document SOS and those of the major library binderies are available, and subscriptions to these, perhaps jointly with the local record office, can be taken out to ensure priority treatment in the event of a disaster. Model plans and forms are also available, for example those drawn up by the East Midlands Museum Service.

B6.2 Stock management

➤ In local studies certain aspects of stock management require special care and attention. These include the management of branch collections, donations and duplicate material.

B6.2.1 Branch collections

➤ The maintenance of satellite local studies collections in branch or community libraries is an important part of the work of the local studies librarian.

Branch collections will consist partly of purchased material, and partly of copies of items gathered by the community. It is essential that the content of branch collections is monitored by the local studies department to ensure a balance appropriate to the particular locality. They should include extensive collections of extracted cuttings and documents, perhaps in the 'parish pack' format in binders, as described by Bromwich (1987), or alternatively as individual indexed and laminated documents, stored in filing boxes. Branch or community libraries require an adequate supply of titles relating to the local area, and will also find that resources such as albums of photographs or files of cuttings are of considerable value and the subject of great interest at local level. Original items received by donation at subsidiary service points should be forwarded to the local studies department for a decision about their permanent location. This must take account of the donor's expressed preference, but in most instances the originals will be retained in the central collection, with copies made for branch collections where appropriate. Mobile library services should not be overlooked, as a useful link with small or rural communities, and indeed a specialized 'History Van' has been a feature in Birmingham (See *Local Studies Librarian*, **13** (1), Summer 1994).

B6.2.2 Donations

➤ Local studies libraries should have a written policy on donations, for the guidance of both staff and prospective donors.

Individuals and organizations will often express their appreciation of the value of the local studies library by offering donations or making bequests, ranging in size from single items to substantial collections. However, prospective donors should always be made aware of the conditions under which larger donations or bequests are accepted. These can form the basis of a written agreement between parties. The following points should be covered:

- Selection. Will the library be able to select items in advance?
- Accessibility. The material will normally be made available to all library users.
- Security. The library should provide a general description of the care to be accorded.
- Listing. The library should undertake to catalogue or list the items in the collection, perhaps within an agreed time limit.
- Disposal. The library may wish to reserve powers to dispose of surplus material by transfer or sale.
- Permanence. Most libraries will only accept material as an outright gift, but some now adopt the archivist's practice of accepting collections on temporary or semi-permanent deposit.
- Rights. What rights will accrue to the library and which of them will be retained by the donor? Is the donor in a position to assign copyright? If the library has an active publishing and/or digitization programme such rights are of considerable significance.

B6.2.3 Duplicate material

➤ Libraries must draw up well-considered guidelines for the disposal of surplus material.

Local studies libraries will usually retain duplicate copies of most items, either to safeguard the needs of future generations against loss or damage, or for branch library reference or lending use. However, there may be occasions when material can be disposed of by means of gift or sale. For example, a donation or bequest can result in a large number of duplicate items. When disposal is decided upon, it is suggested that the guidelines for disposal drawn up by the Library Association Rare Book Group be carefully followed. For example, it should be checked that the library has the authority to sell the items in question, and also that the copies are genuinely duplicate and not association copies, copies with significant annotations, or variant editions. The library should clarify its reasons for the disposal, also what it intends to do with any income. It should be recognized that considerable expense is involved in preparing material for disposal, and documenting what has been disposed of. Because of the special nature of local studies collections the decision to dispose of items should never be taken lightly.

B6.3   Classification and cataloguing

> ➤ Local studies collections should be catalogued and indexed using systems that reflect the requirements of their special nature.

The cataloguing of local studies material presents special problems, which cannot always be addressed by central cataloguing services. The cataloguer of the local studies collection cannot always download acceptable records from remote databases, and is frequently in the position of needing to construct the authoritative record for the national published archive. Cataloguing should therefore be detailed, with adequate bibliographical description to AACR standards, with provenance and acquisition information for unique and unpublished items and for copies with special features such as extra-illustration or annotations. Details relevant to the usage of items, such as remote storage, fragility, intellectual property rights and other restrictions on access should also be noted where appropriate. Analytical records for especially significant sections of works should be made where required.

The cataloguer should have sufficient awareness of the history of printing to be able to assign dates to undated items and to differentiate between the various methods of reproduction of text and illustrations.

A number of local studies classification schemes and many adaptations of other more general schemes have been devised, but few have found widespread use. Any scheme employed for open access collections or in a classified subject catalogue should be devised with ease of use by readers in mind. On this basis, a modification of a widely used classification scheme, especially Dewey, should be seriously considered.

With the growing use of keyword searching, the importance of classified arrangement in closed access collections and for non-book materials is diminished. In such circumstances, preservation of the integrity of arrangement of special and historic collections is more readily possible.

Some local studies materials, such as ephemera, may be more amenable to archival listing, perhaps at collection or group level, rather than to traditional library cataloguing and classification. Subject indexing should ensure access to items by place, subject, individual name and date. Subject headings should be devised in such a way that similar search strategies can be undertaken not only in the main monograph catalogue but also in the various special indexes to photographs, 35mm slides, periodical articles, cuttings, scrapbooks, ephemera, oral history collections and other materials that need to be devised for local studies collections. Such consistency will make the production of an integrated collection database easier when computerization takes place.

The development of a hierarchical thesaurus can lead to more consistency in indexing, cope with the wide range of specialist terms encountered in local studies work and help to group items for subject searching on computerized indexing systems. It may be fruitful to discuss the development of a common thesaurus with the local record office.

B6.3.1 Digitizing the catalogue

➤ Schemes for the computerization of library catalogues should include a fully integrated scheme for cataloguing local studies collections held within the service, including branch collections and collections of non-book materials, such as press cuttings, prints, maps and architectural drawings.

The system should be capable of communicating through networks and being searched remotely using Z39.50 and other protocols. It should be capable of handling detailed records of material in a wide variety of formats, including copy-specific information, in an integrated file with links to digitized images and text where appropriate. Searching should be possible by place, subject, proper name and date range, as well as by author and title.

Because of the specialized nature of local studies catalogue entries, and the permanence of local studies items within the collection, it may not be appropriate to include such items in the main library stock management system, although the facility to provide ready information relating to ordering, acquisition, binding and conservation is helpful. By the same token, loans modules are not necessarily required for the local studies collection, but the facility for recording special loans for such purposes as photography, conservation and exhibitions can be useful. If a separate stock management system is employed for local studies there should be the facility to move records between systems.

Interfaces for staff adding and editing data and for members of the public searching the database should be user friendly, with text prompts as well as icons. Help texts can include background information relevant to the different types of sources. Printout and other report-generating facilities greatly enhance the usefulness of the catalogue.

Preparation can begin well before a suitable stock management system is fully acquired. In Devon a basic record structure suitable for a wide range of document types was devised during the mid-1980s and was used for more than 15 years on versions of d-Base customized in-house. By 1999 there were 65,000 monograph records and separate databases for periodical articles and illustrations. From 1986 the databases were used to generate the annual *Devon Bibliography*, a web-based catalogue, and web pages for individual scanned images. The option of migrating the data onto a networked stock management system was part of the plan from the outset (See Maxted, *Local Studies Librarian*, **16** (1), Summer 1997).

Wherever possible, integration with the catalogues of appropriate record offices, museums and special libraries should be investigated.

B6.4 Digitizing the collection

➤ The digitization of collections is essential in the modern library world. Involvement in projects to digitize materials in the local collection is nowadays a regular part of the duties of the local studies librarian.

Such projects fulfil the commitment of the *New Library* report to make local materials more readily available, and indeed contribute in an important way to the national library of digitized materials. This in turn can be seen as having potential for the National Grid for Learning, as suggested in DoEE, *Connecting the Learning Society* (1997). To maximize the effectiveness of this contribution, it is important that Local Studies Libraries keep in touch with national priorities for digitization. However, the requirements of national projects should be balanced against regional and local needs. At local level the fragile nature of original materials can be an important factor when setting priorities for digitization, perhaps equally with subject and/or educational demand. The preparation of digital copies is an excellent means of protecting rare and fragile materials from loss or damage.

Images should be archived and made accessible in standard cross-platform formats. At least two levels of digitization may be required: i.e. high-resolution images as masters for quality reproduction and smaller compressed images for speed of loading on networks and to deter copyright theft and unauthorized usage.

Digitization of images should be carried out by means of a high grade digital camera. If library resources do not accommodate the provision of such a camera, the services of a digitization bureau should be employed. Such bureaux often prefer to work with 35mm negatives and slides, rather than photographs; 35mm film can in any case be seen as an effective intermediary for digitization, at the same time providing an archivally proven surrogate. Surrogate images should always be properly catalogued.

During the 1990s a number of local authorities developed ambitious schemes for the digitization of local materials held in libraries, museums and archives. A descriptive list was published in the *Virtually new* report (Parry), prepared by Information North for the Library and Information Commission and published in 1998. Most schemes were for the straightforward digitization of photographic images, but a few were considerably more ambitious than that. The Durham Record, commenced in 1994, was the first system to offer full public access (on standalone PCs with touch screens) to an integrated database of modern and historic maps and photographs. High quality printouts were available and the system also included archaeological records, thereby providing an example of how textual material could be linked to visual images and maps. The 'Hackney on Disc' system, developed by Hackney Archives Department and Local Studies Library from 1994 onwards, embraced catalogue records, photographs and historic Ordnance Survey mapping. The 'Hackney on Disc' software was packaged for commercial distribution, offering a facility for database creation, scanning, map calibration, and location of images on maps. The 'Knowsley Local History' website, created in 1997-8 by means of a Wolfson Public Libraries Challenge Fund award, was a pioneer example of how a digitized historical guide to a moderately-sized community could be created fairly rapidly (in just three months in Knowsley's case), given adequate resources of funding and the necessary commitment (**history.knowsley.gov.uk/browse_kv. html**).

The Scottish Cultural Resources Access Network (SCRAN) project was begun in 1996, as a lottery-funded scheme to create a website embracing 1.5 million digitized records of Scottish artefacts, buildings and sites. The National Museums of Scotland was one of the founding partners, so the scheme has been largely museum-orientated, but a number of Scottish local studies libraries have contributed images of photographs and prints from their collections. An important feature of SCRAN is the discipline it imposes on the provision of adequate descriptive text to support the digitized images. It has set the standard for future development of a Scottish national resource base of digitized cultural images.

Digitization covers text as well as images, including the associated texts that bring individual images to life. The New Opportunities Fund digitization programme has required a uniformity of approach on the part of libraries throughout the UK, and in so doing has gone some way towards the setting of standards for future content creation. The nof-digitise technical standards cover accessibility, availability, document and file formats, search and request protocols, security and e-commerce, preservation and metadata (**www.peoplesnetwork.gov.uk/nof/technicalstandards.html**).

B6.4.1 Networking

➤ Local studies libraries should develop programmes for systematic digitization of local content for the national network.

Priorities for the creation of content for the New Library Network were laid down by the Library and Information Commission in *Building the New Library Network* (1998), in terms of the government's stated social, educational and economic policy objectives. These were 'cultural enrichment', 'the modernisation of government and the encouragement of active citizenship' and 'reskilling the nation to meet the challenge of an information society'. Appropriate themes within the 'cultural enrichment' objective were suggested as:

- Our digital heritage: local regional and national history expressed in characteristic objects, artefacts and archives selectively themed and presented with research findings, analysis and cross-referenced background in a way that will permit interpretation and enjoyment at different levels of abilities.
- Our community identity: local histories brought together from across the UK to form a rich patchwork of personal and community identity in map and manuscript, photograph and archive film, voice and other sound recordings.
- Our creative experience: the story of UK creative experience in the visual and fine arts, fashion and design, architecture, film, television and the media – all as represented in the collections, resources, expertise and activities of cultural institutions, learned societies, arts bodies, libraries and community art centres.

New Opportunities Fund support for the creation of 'cultural' content would be according to these themes.

Building the New Library Network also laid down the anticipated balance between Local, Regional and National themed material for the New Library Network. Fifteen percent of resources would be targeted at projects with a local focus but with potential for national interest. Material of local focus but 'no national interest' would not receive New Opportunities Fund support.

It is clearly very difficult to establish criteria to determine whether or not local material possesses any 'national interest'. Virtually all of the material held in local studies collections will be subject to external interest at some time or other, whether by subject specialists seeking local material for comparative or illustrative purposes, or students of genealogy or family history wishing to return to their roots. Local studies librarians will therefore seek to find other sources of funding for the digitization of local materials failing to meet the NOF criteria. They should remember that grant applications are more likely to succeed if framed as joint bids with museums, record offices or other outside organizations. More permanent sources of funding will in any case be necessary. It is essential that the problem of 'sustainability' be addressed, and every effort be made to ensure that sufficient funding is available in the longer term. Adequate funding is also vital in the short term as 'matching funding' for grant applications.

Local studies librarians will make use of a wide range of networked information, from a variety of external sources. For example a massive amount of family history is now available on the internet. Some regional newspapers are now providing subscription services to their indexed files online, as an alternative to CD-ROM provision. For example, the *Belfast Telegraph* is available as an online archive, retrospective to November 1995, by means of an 'electronic library card', with the option of an annual subscription or access to a specified number of features (**www. belfasttelegraph.co.uk/archive/**).

Local studies librarians must be fully aware of relevant online services and be able to provide assistance in their use.

B6.4.2 Metadata

> ➤ Images and other material digitized for network use should be supported by adequate metadata.

Many systems for creating metadata are available, so a great deal of care is required when making a choice. The option of sticking with well established library cataloguing procedures, including MARC records and AACR2, has much to commend it, because it includes the facility for incorporating extensive detail, control over subject headings and Z39.50 interoperability. There are emerging standards for metadata, and the adoption of the Dublin Core by the UK government in 2000 (Cabinet Office, *e-government interoperability framework*) may be seen as a significant factor in this. Various initiatives seek to arrive at a convergence in item description that could bridge the requirements of libraries, archives, museums and other information resources. Regardless of the system in use, special care should be taken with standards of data entry. For example the Online Computer Library Centre (OCLC) has developed the CORC (Co-operative Online Resource Catalogue) system of cataloguing, specifically for digitized resources on the internet. CORC supports records created in MARC/AACR2 and also those created in the simpler Dublin Core system. Records can be exported in either format or in an XML encoding – increasingly an important format. The flexibility of CORC would seem to recommend it as a suitable cataloguing system for digitized local studies resources.

B6.5 Income generation

➤ Local studies staff should be able to exploit the potential of local studies resources to provide income that can be applied to develop the collections.

Some aspects of local studies librarianship lend themselves to income generation; levying of reproduction fees or royalties, provision of genealogical services and the publication and sale of such items as local calendars and greetings cards are examples. When these activities become part of the work of the local studies department it is essential that adequate staffing and accommodation are made available for the purpose. Care should also be taken to recycle income from such sources towards development of the local studies collection/service.

Some libraries favour a policy of building in a substantial profit margin, when supplying copy photographs, 35 mm slides, etc. to members of the public and/or the local business community. Birmingham Central Library, for example, charges British Association of Picture Libraries and Agencies (BAPLA) rates for commercial provision of photographs. The supply of bygone local views for display on the walls of public houses, restaurants, offices, rest homes etc. can often be a source of considerable income. Other libraries consider the supply of copy photographs to be primarily a public service and therefore retain only a small profit, if any at all. It should be remembered that many donors of photographs to library collections make them available on the understanding that they should be fully accessible to all, with a minimum of restriction.

Some libraries are able to offer fee-based research services for the benefit of enquirers who for various reasons may be unable to carry out their own investigations. Charging for such services should ideally be co-ordinated with the local record office to prevent anomalous variation. If income-generating research is undertaken, care must be taken to protect the existing free service to users who visit the library to carry out their own local or genealogical research. This free service should include personal help from staff to a degree comparable with assistance given to other library users.

B6.6 Publishing

➤ Local studies libraries should be prepared to develop a publishing programme to improve access to local studies information.

The publishing of local history material can be financially advantageous to the library service, but this should not be regarded as the principal motive for going into print. The first responsibility of the local studies library is to produce a guide or set of guides to its own collections. Once this is achieved, it is nowadays common to undertake the publishing of local texts and documents, an activity that can be regarded as a logical development from the library's mainstream lending and reference functions. Library publishing facilitates the widespread circulation of useful local material that might not be viable for a commercial publisher to handle, especially in areas of low population. New titles extend the range of knowledge available and so are often considered to be of greater priority for attention than reprints of standard histories. The local studies librarian is in a good position to survey the existing range of literature, to identify gaps and begin to fill them by means of a publishing programme, which can be planned in a systematic way, over several years. Accordingly, the local studies librarian is sometimes given full responsibility for organizing this activity, although some libraries favour the appointment of a publications working group to spread the workload and provide a wider perspective.

B6.6.1 Staffing requirements

➤ The implications of a publishing programme in terms of staff must be considered when the programme is being planned.

The marketing of publications, for example, is extremely time consuming, but nevertheless essential. Although library staff may often be willing to help with the preparation of text or to devote time to the technical aspects of publication, such commitment must be fully recognized by the senior library manager as part of the job and not taken for granted as some kind of personal enthusiasm.

B6.6.2 Bibliographical standards

➤ No library should produce a book that falls below accepted standards of bibliographical competence.

Care must be taken to provide the name of the publisher, date, and correct and adequate bibliographical information in references and bibliographies etc. A planned house-style is helpful in the systematic maintenance of good standards of production. When publishing local studies material, the use of acid-free paper is desirable, to ensure permanence.

B6.6.3 Authors

> ➤ The best possible author in a subject field should always be sought for a publication initiated by the library service.

The local studies librarian is often in a good position to identify suitable authors. These might include 'lifelong learning' students, who sometimes target gaps in the local bibliography when deciding on subjects suitable for dissertations and theses. Commissioned authors should always be paid a publication royalty or fee.

B6.6.4 Pricing

> ➤ Care should be taken to set the price of library publications at a realistic level.

The principal elements of the sale price will be: unit cost (including design and printing costs and author's royalty); distributor's fee; bookshop mark-up; and library profit margin. The price should be set at a level the market will bear, but care should be taken to avoid loss-making ventures.

B6.6.5 Electronic publishing

> ➤ Local studies librarians should be prepared to investigate the option of electronic publishing, instead of print.

If the use of a library website is available, the possibility of publishing online can be considered. This will require a lower level of outlay than full print publishing, but will not generate income in the same way. However, it is worthy of consideration for useful titles of low market potential. On occasion the simultaneous publication of print and online versions is appropriate. Certain titles might also be suitable for publication in CD-ROM format.

B6.6.6 Postcard publishing

> ➤ The publication of postcards should be regarded as a valid activity, as a means of making visual material from the library's collections more widely available, while at the same time reducing wear and tear on the originals.

B6.6.7 Educational publishing

> ➤ Publication of local studies material in a form designed for school use is a means of increasing the usefulness of the local collection to the educational world.

School curricula nowadays require the use of local source material by pupils, often resulting in over-use of rare or important resources. Special reproduction of material for teaching purposes is a way of alleviating this problem, as well as providing an opportunity for constructive links between the teaching profession and the local studies library.

B6.7 Intellectual property

➤ Local studies librarians must be aware of the implications of copyright and other intellectual property rights.

B6.7.1 Copyright

➤ It is essential that the local studies librarian acquire a good knowledge of copyright law.

Where appropriate, expert advice should be taken on matters such as the copyright of commissioned photographs, authors' rights with regard to works published by the library and, very importantly, the procedures necessary to authorize multiple copies for classroom use. The relevant legislation is contained in the Copyright, Designs and Patents Act, 1988, supplemented by the Duration of Copyright and Rights of Performances Regulations 1995, SI 1995: 3297 (which takes in the European dimension).

B6.7.2 Right of access

➤ Libraries can levy a fee for use of material from library stock by authors, publishers, broadcasters, compilers of educational packages and other commercial interests.

This should be regarded as a 'right of access' fee and should not be confused with copyright payments. 'Right of access' cannot be granted in this way to items still held in unexpired copyright by external agencies or individuals. Some libraries also derive income from copyright fees for media use of material from library publications, photographs taken by library staff as part of local surveys, and other items for which the library holds full copyright.

B7 Staff

> Every public library authority should have a local studies department, headed by a local studies librarian.

The local studies librarian should have responsibility for the supervision of local studies collections and services in all libraries of the local authority. Because of the specialist nature of the work an appropriately experienced member of staff should be assigned to this post.

B7.1 The local studies librarian

> The local studies post should carry the designation of local studies librarian and should be structured at a reasonably senior level in the library management hierarchy.

The range and complexity of local studies work and the high profile of local studies in the community might even provide a case for inclusion of the local studies librarian in the senior management team. The local studies librarian should have full professional qualifications, and should either have completed a course on local studies work as part of his/her qualifying examinations, or be able to demonstrate that he/she has attended other formal courses appropriate to his/her special duties as local studies librarian. It should also be recognized that experience is of particular importance in the local studies library where it can take a considerable period of time to acquire full knowledge of the wide range of resources available.

The local studies librarian should have the following experience, skills and competencies:

- Detailed knowledge of local studies resources, both internal and external.
- Knowledge of guidelines/standards in local studies and related fields such as archives and museum curatorship.
- Experience of working with the public.
- Ability to work with related professions.
- Ability to work with relevant community groups.
- Customer care skills.
- Public speaking skills.
- Effective written and oral communication skills.
- Editorial and bibliographical skills.
- Organizational skills.

- Management skills.
- Teaching skills, to promote effective library use.
- Promotional skills.
- Competence in working with ICT.
- Enthusiasm for local and family history.
- Understanding of users' needs.

If local studies resources are to be fully publicized and exploited, the local studies librarian must maintain active links with relevant societies. It should be recognized that such societies invariably meet during evenings or at weekends, and that the local studies librarian will therefore be required to work flexible hours. Such work should be regarded as part of the normal duties of the local studies librarian, and recompense in time or payment be made accordingly. It should not be regarded as spare time or voluntary activity. However, if local organizations offer remuneration for talks provided in 'library time', clearly such sums of money should either be politely refused or returned to library funds.

In situations where local staffing levels cannot accommodate a full-time local studies librarian, the senior reference librarian should be entrusted with oversight of the local studies service, which should always be recognized as one of the more important and valued areas of reference work.

B7.2 Supporting staff

➤ Additional local studies staff should be provided in sufficient numbers to oversee public access to the collection effectively, to answer routine enquiries and to enable satisfactory standards in the acquisition, cataloguing and indexing of local studies items to be maintained.

All members of the local studies staff should possess a reasonable proportion of the attributes expected of a local studies librarian (listed in **B7.1** above). Customer care skills and a willingness to develop personal knowledge of local studies are of prime importance.

B7.3 Training

➤ The training of all library staff in the range of services provided by the local studies service is essential.

- There should be an ongoing programme of training courses, organized by the local studies librarian, to promote awareness of appropriate techniques.
- Local studies should be included in the induction training of new library staff.
- Specialist local studies staff should receive comprehensive training in the work of the section, and should attend external courses to update their

professional skills.

- Frontline staff are often the first to be consulted when a member of the public enters the local studies library, and should accordingly receive careful training in assistance to readers and the answering of quick reference enquiries.
- Training in customer care and telephone skills is essential.
- Senior local studies staff should receive training in management techniques, also organizational and promotional skills.
- The external training of senior local studies staff should include courses providing an awareness of museum and archive practice, also the work of other local authority departments.
- Temporary exchanges of staff with museums and record offices will provide useful insight for all concerned.
- Care should be taken to allocate sufficient time for training purposes.

B7.4   Volunteers and friends groups

➤ The local studies service should harness and make use of the enthusiasm of volunteers, wherever possible.

There is a wide range of ways in which volunteers can assist with the work of the local studies library, from the individual researcher who makes his/her indexes available to the library, to the team of volunteers that offers to assist with the accomplishment of funded projects. If a 'Friends of the Library' group exists in the local area, the members will often find that involvement in local studies projects serves as a natural outlet for their enthusiasm and commitment. Such help should be welcomed – it has for long been a mainstay of the museum sector – but it should be remembered that volunteers might require careful supervision. Staff time must be available for the purpose. While formal contracts and recruiting procedures are not always appropriate, there are instances where those may be necessary, and in any case volunteers should receive sufficient training to ensure that their work is of genuine value to the local studies service. Trade unions should be consulted before volunteers are formally employed, and volunteers should never be used to compensate for the reduction or withdrawal of staff from the full-time establishment. Non-core duties appropriate to volunteers include:

- Listing the contents of collections.
- Indexing newspapers.
- Cleaning stock.
- Routine conservation duties, such as the substitution of archival boxes/folders/envelopes for their non-archival equivalents.
- Preparing material for displays.

The Library Association report on *The use of volunteers in public libraries* (2000) is useful as a guideline, although perhaps too formal for some of the ad hoc situations that can arise in the local studies library.

B8 Facilities management

B8.1 Accommodation

➤ The physical location of areas designed to house local studies collections should always be carefully planned.

When library buildings are constructed or adapted the opportunity should be taken to provide accommodation of the highest standard, professionally space-planned, in consultation with the local studies librarian.

B8.1.1 Public study areas

➤ Areas designated for use by members of the public should be planned with both security and user convenience in mind. Considerations include:

- Design that allows for careful supervision of readers consulting irreplace-able materials.
- Adequate seating.
- Generous provision of large tables for consultation of maps, plans, broad-sheet newspapers, newspaper volumes, and other large items.
- Space for specialist equipment such as computers, microform readers and printers. Special ICT areas are sometimes appropriate, with sufficient power and telecommunications points.
- Purpose-designed desks and adjustable chairs for use with specialist equipment.
- Lighting levels that protect documents from over-intense exposure, and that permit the use of microforms without eye strain.
- Sound-proof carrels for the use of oral history tapes and other sound archives.
- A display area to promote the range of material in the collection.
- Location of photocopiers to minimize noise and disruption, but also to ensure the security of items copied.
- Adequate access and user facilities for the disabled.

B8.1.2 Storage areas

➤ Secure storage must be provided and should be located close to the public study areas, but with adequate controls to prevent entry by members of the public.

Provision within the stores should include specialist shelving and furniture, such as non-standard sizes of shelving (including closely-mounted shelving of appropriate length for horizontal storage of single newspaper volumes), map cabinets and microform cabinets, large format filing cabinets, and a large safe. A separate filing area for unbound copies of local newspapers and periodicals is desirable. Smoke detectors should be installed, and fire escape routes be planned to avoid public egress through the stores. Service pipes, for water etc., should not be routed through the stores. Inappropriate electrical or heating appliances should not be located here. Equipment should be installed to maintain the correct environmental conditions (temperature and humidity) for the different types of local studies resource material, as outlined in BS5454 *Storage and exhibition of archival documents*. Table top surfaces should be generously provided, to facilitate the handling and sorting of materials. There should be constant appraisal of space required for future expansion of stock.

B8.1.3 Office accommodation

➤ There should be adequate office accommodation for members of the local studies staff.

Ideally, each member of staff should have his/her own work station, equipped with a PC, copystand, adjacent shelving etc. There should be adequate table-top space for items of equipment such as mounting presses, laminators and guillotines, appropriate shelving for accommodation of newly-received local studies materials and resources of all kinds, and storage cupboards for archival and other specialist stationery.

B8.1.4 Open access provision

➤ If at all possible, a moderate collection of local studies books and other materials should be provided on 'open access'.

This will be much appreciated by researchers, and indeed some library users come into the local studies department simply for the pleasure of browsing among the local studies materials. Clearly, unique material should never be put at risk, but duplicate copies can be purchased as funds allow, sometimes even out-of-print items from specialist sources, and bound photocopies of rarer material can be prepared, to enable the development of an open-access section. If an open-access collection is provided, appropriate shelving, filing cabinets, etc. will require to be provided in the public study area, and space made available to accommodate these.

B8.2 Equipment

➤ Staff should be aware of the special requirements of equipment purchased for the local studies library.

When purchasing equipment there should be careful study of the latest editions of trade catalogues of library and other specialist suppliers, to check what is available for the intended purpose, from the point of view of both suitability and price. Safety is also a prime consideration, and consultation with Council health and safety officers will sometimes be necessary, although this will more often take place during installation. Certain types of map storage cabinet, for example, require to be bolted into position, to prevent them from tilting forwards in a dangerous manner during use.

B8.2.1 Storage equipment

➤ Care should be taken to acquire appropriate storage equipment for special materials such as maps, microforms, photographs, negatives, 35mm transparencies, ephemera etc.

As part of the same process, a supply of the correct archival stationery should be acquired for storage of each category, including various types of acid-free boxes, folders and envelopes, and polyester sleeves. Some of these can be expensive, but cost should not be a prohibiting factor when the correct storage of irreplaceable items is under consideration. Materials likely to cause damage to documents, such as conventional adhesive tape, double-sided adhesive tape and PVC, should be carefully avoided. Advice should be sought from professional conservators, where appropriate.

B8.2.2 Microform readers

➤ A range of microform readers is an essential provision in the local studies library.

Despite the rapid increase in digital alternatives, material in microform is still in great demand. Newspaper files are held extensively on microform, and local record offices are increasingly involved in microfilming projects of which libraries can take advantage. Film of census enumerators' returns is now widely held by libraries and heavily used by family historians and genealogists; genealogical research has also prompted acquisition of microform material such as the *International Genealogical Index*, the Name Index to the 1881 Census, and the General Register Office index of births, marriages and deaths. It should be recognized that an adequate number of good quality microform readers and reader-printers needs to be provided for the use of this material; expenditure on the acquisition of the microforms has often been considerable, and expenditure on the associated equipment should be undertaken as necessary for its full exploitation. Maintenance of such equipment in good condition is essential, and many libraries find it expedient to take out a maintenance contract. The greatest of care should be taken in the selection of these, especially as they are often expensive. The use of microfilm readers capable of producing digital copies can provide an effective link between traditional microforms and full digital environments.

B8.2.3 Photocopiers

➤ Photocopiers have many essential uses in the local studies library.

Photocopying equipment is now universally available for both staff and public use, and indeed many libraries now have colour copiers (although not always in the local studies department). In the local studies library photocopiers are frequently employed to make copies of rare and/or fragile material to save wear and tear of the originals. Copies should never be made, however, if this would cause damage to the originals – for example, if a volume is too heavy to lift comfortably, or if material would need to be bent or folded.

A wide range of equipment for provision of digital copies is now available, embracing copiers, scanners and digital cameras, and increasingly library users expect inexpensive digital copies of illustrative material to be available as a matter of course. Specialist advice should be sought when choosing digital copying equipment, for use in the local studies library (*see also* **B5.1.5** above).

All members of the library staff should be made aware of the damage that careless photocopying can cause. They should be given guidance as to what can be copied safely, and should be supported in any decision to disallow the photocopying of an item for a reader if this would be detrimental to its conservation. Alternative methods for copying documents include scanners, digital cameras and flat bed photocopiers (all of which, if available, are less likely to damage originals). All staff should be given training in copyright legislation, especially with regard to the potential for abuse of photocopy equipment in this respect.

B8.2.4 Photographic equipment

➤ The purchase of a good range of photographic equipment should be given careful consideration.

Unless the services of a library photographic department are available, a good quality camera can be a very useful tool in the local studies library, both for copying photographs and for record photography, and should be provided whenever financial resources allow. For copying photographs a copy stand, with appropriate lighting fitments, is also required.

B8.2.5 Sound and video recorders

➤ Equipment to play oral recordings and portable recorders for use in oral history projects are desirable for the local studies library.

Reel-to-reel recorders are required for use with sound archives, and cassette recorders are often still employed for field work. However, minidisc systems are now in general use, with portable minidisc recorders employed for oral history recording sessions. Care is required when purchasing minidisc equipment, as many options are available, some of them unsuitable for the generation of material for oral history archives. In general, expert help should always be sought when purchasing such equipment. Most local studies libraries hold collections of local videos, and will require a VCR and TV monitor to make those available for consultation by library users. Digital video equipment is now in widespread use, but again advice should be sought when making purchases.

B8.2.6 Computers

➤ A range of computers and other ICT equipment, for both staff and public use, is vital in the modern local studies library.

The purchase of such equipment will often require a greater degree of deliberation than does the acquisition of other library equipment, because of its fundamental importance at the present time, and the enormous range of options on offer. Specifications should conform to the ICT standards adopted by the local authority as a whole, especially as this will often be necessary to ensure adequate technical support. In the local studies department users should expect direct access to networked PCs to view library catalogues and CD-ROMs, as well as appropriate information on the internet. It may also be helpful to allow PCs to be used for word-processing or database input of information obtained from the collections. Good quality laser and other printers should always be provided, including those with colour printing facility. Facilities for users to work with their own laptop computers should also be available. Mediated or direct access to scanners, digital cameras and digital recorders may also be required. The use of digital cameras to capture pages can sometimes be effective where works cannot be photocopied or scanned. The value of computers in the presentation of sound and video information should be recognized, and there may be a requirement for headphones or carrels for listening and/or viewing. Space and staffing constraints may mean that such resources cannot be maintained within the library and users may have to be encouraged to use digital resources remotely. For these reasons it is important that there is access to a CD/DVD writer so that textual, visual, sound and moving image resources can be copied for external use, always provided that copyright and other rights issues are borne in mind. Staff would also be able to copy data offered to the library in CD-ROM format. ICT can revolutionize the exchange of local studies information, and it is vital that local studies libraries participate fully in these exciting developments.

Bibliography

The following Bibliography was drawn up specifically to accompany the present *Guidelines*. For a more comprehensive listing of works relating to local studies, which was compiled for the Local Studies Group, *see*:

Dixon, Diana (2001) *Local studies librarianship: a world bibliography*, Library Association Publishing.

A1 The service

Cave, Roderick (1982) *Rare book librarianship*, 2nd edn, Bingley.

COSLA (1995) *Standards for the public library service in Scotland 1995*, COSLA.

Department for Culture, Media and Sport (2001) *Comprehensive, efficient and modern public libraries - standards and assessment*, DCMS, available at **www.culture.gov.uk/PDF/libraries_pls_assess.pdf**

Dewe, Michael (ed.) (1991) *Local studies collections: a manual*, vol. 2, Gower.

Dewe, Michael (ed.) (1987) *Manual of local studies librarianship*, vol. 1, Gower.

Guy, Susanna (1992) *English local studies handbook*, University of Exeter.

Harris, Richard, Feather, John and Evans, Margaret (2000) *The legal deposit of local publications: a case study of Leicestershire, Leicester and Rutland*, Library and Information Commission.

Hobbs, J. L. (1973) *Local history and the library 1962*, Deutsch. Completely revised by George A. Carter.
Includes a suggested classification scheme for local studies.

Library Association, Information Services Group (1999) *Guidelines for reference and information services in public libraries*, Library Association Publishing.

Library Association (2000) *Libraries and lifelong learning: Library Association policy*, LA, available at **www.la-hq.org.uk/directory/prof.issues/lip.html**

Lomax, Joanne et al. (1997) *A guide to additional sources of funding and revenue for libraries and archives*, British Library and Information Research Report 108.

Lynes, Alice (1974) *How to organise a local collection*, Deutsch.

National Preservation Office (1999) *The application and use of standards in the care and management of libraries and archives*, NPO.

New Library: the people's network (1997) Library and Information Commission for Department of Culture, Media and Sport. Published as a command paper CM 3887, 1998, available at **www.ukoln.ac.uk/services/lic/newlibrary/full.html**

Nichols, Harold (1979) *Local studies librarianship*, Bingley.

Parry, David (1998) *Virtually new. Creating the digital collection. A review of digitisation projects in local authority libraries and archives. A report to the Library and Information Commission by Information North*, Information North, available at

www.ukoln.ac.uk/services/lic/digitisation

Phillips, Faye (1995) *Local history collections in libraries*, Libraries Unlimited.

Scottish Library and Information Council (1999) *Implementing Best Value in public library services: a tool kit for performance management*, SLIC.

Society of Archivists (1993) *Best practice guideline No 1: Measuring performance*, Society of Archivists.

Recommends measurement of cataloguing work as well as user satisfaction.

Thomas, Anita (2001) Planning for Best Value in local studies, *Local Studies Librarian* **20** (2), 7–10.

Winterbotham, Diana and Crosby, Alan (1999) *The local studies library*, BALH.

A2 The user

Baird, Patrick (1993) Genealogy workshops in Birmingham, *Local Studies Librarian*, **12** (2), 20.

Black and Asian Studies Association Newsletter, published three times a year (formerly Association for the Study of African, Caribbean and Asian Culture and History in Britain newsletter), issue 1, September 1991.

Bray, Joan (2000) Equal opportunities and local studies, *Local Studies Librarian* **19** (1), 6–9.

Cooke, Sheila (1992) Local studies and the multi-cultural community, *Local Studies Librarian*, **11** (1), 3–5.

Department for Culture, Media and Sport (2000) *Centres for social change: museums, galleries and archives*, DCMS, available at
www.culture.gov.uk/heritage/social_change.html

Department for Culture, Media and Sport (1999) *Libraries for all: social inclusion in public libraries*, DCMS, available at
www.culture.gov.uk/heritage/lib1.html

Duffin, P. (1992) *Then and now: a training pack for reminiscence work*, Gatehouse.

Gibson, Faith (1994) *Reminiscence and recall: a guide to good practice*, Ace Books.

Library and Information Commission (2000) *Libraries: the essence of inclusion*, LIC, available at
www.lic.gov.uk/publications/policyreports/inclusion.html

Library Association, Information Services Group (1999) *Guidelines for reference and information services in public libraries*, Library Association Publishing.

Library Association, Youth Libraries Committee (1997) *Children and young people: Library Association guidelines for public library services*, Library Association Publishing.

Matkin, C. and Gordon, R. A. (2000) Consulting the customers: a survey of local studies library users in Derby and Derbyshire, *Local Studies Librarian*, **19** (1), 2–5.

Petty, Mike (1996) Networking local studies, *Local Studies Librarian*, **15** (1), 2–5.

Sharp, D. C. (1989) *Public library provision of a local studies service in a multi ethnic society: a review to assist further discussion*, Leeds Polytechnic Department of Library and Information Studies, M A occasional publication no. 5.

Timmins, Geoff (1992) Local history teaching and the national curriculum, *Local Studies Librarian*, **11** (1), 16–18.

Usherwood, Bob (1999) The social impact of local studies services, *Local Studies Librarian*, **18** (1), 2–6.

A3   Relationships

Association of Metropolitan Authorities (1994) *Preserving past, present and future*, Association of Metropolitan Authorities.

Foster, Janet and Sheppard, Julia (1995) *British archives: a guide to archive sources in the United Kingdom*, 3rd edn, Macmillan.

Guide to the Parochial Registers and Records Measure 1978 as amended at 1 January 1993 with practical suggestions for custodians and users (1992), 2nd edn, Church House Publishing.

Hayes, Martin (1997) Sleeping with the enemy: co-operation between archivists and librarians in West Sussex, *Local Studies Librarian*, **16** (1), 2–5.

Knightbridge, A. A. H. (1985) *Archive legislation in the UK Society of Archivists*, Information leaflet 3, Society of Archivists.
Describes legislation for care of public, ecclesiastical, manorial and business records and position in Scotland and Northern Ireland (but somewhat out of date).

Royal Commission on Historical Manuscripts (1997) *A standard for record repositories on constitution, finance, staff, acquisition, access*, 2nd edn, RCHM.

Royal Commission on Historical Manuscripts (1999) *Record repositories in Great Britain*, 11th edn, RCHM.

Shaw, Susan (1994) *Beyond the PRO: public records in places of deposit*, Public Record Office.
Summary of laws applying to public records and useful descriptions of minimum storage, public facilities standards and section on resource implications.

A4   Marketing and promotion

Bromwich, David (1987) Parish packs: the Somerset approach, *Local Studies Librarian*, **6** (2), 15–16.

Design a label: guidelines on labelling for museums (1999), Campaign for Museums.

Friggens, Greta (1998) Local studies centres, *Local Studies Librarian*, **17** (2), 8–11.

Hayes, Martin (1995) His sins were scarlet, but his books were read: the work of West Sussex County Council's special events group, *Local Studies Librarian*, **14** (2), 4–9.

Martin, Don (1994) Local studies at the new Kirkintilloch library, *Local Studies Librarian*, **13** (2), 2–4.

Melrose, Elizabeth (1999) Marketing the local studies collection: some observations, *Local Studies Librarian*, **18** (2), 11–15.

Petty, Mike (1983) Working with wireless: some experiences, *Local Studies Librarian*, **2** (2), 17-19.

Petty, Mike (1994) Wake up your potential for promotion, *Local Studies Librarian*, **13** (1), 17-24.

Rimmer, David (1992) Record office or local studies centre, *Journal of the Society of Archivists*, **13** (1), 9-17.

Rimmer, David (1998) Organisation of local studies: a permissive approach, *Local Studies Librarian*, **17** (2), 11-13.

Usherwood, Bob (1999) The social impact of local studies services, *Local Studies Librarian*, **18** (1), 2-6.

B5 The collection

Beare, G. (1999) *Indexing newspapers, magazines and other periodicals*, Society of Indexers.

Bird, Julie (1985) *Oral history collections: their importance in the local history library*, Polytechnic of North London: School of Librarianship and Information Studies, Occasional Publication No. 5.
An abridgement of a final year undergraduate dissertation.

Clinton, Alan (1981) *Printed ephemera: collection, organisation and access*, Clive Bingley.

Collings, J. (1983) *Archival care of still photographs*, Society of Archivists.

Dixon, Diana (2000) Con man or honest broker: three centuries of advertising in the English local newspaper, *Local Studies Librarian*, **19** (1), 12-15.

Fisher, Graham (1993) Thirty Years of the Chester Photographic Survey, *Local Studies Librarian*, **12** (1), 11-13.

Gee, Ralph (1988) Newspaper cuttings – an alternative to indexing? *Local Studies Librarian*, **7** (2), 7-11.

Guidelines for indexing newspapers (1997), Local History Panel of the Library and Information Service Council (Northern Ireland).

Harley, J. B. (1972) *Maps for local historians: a guide to British sources*, National Council of Social Service.

Historian's guide to Ordnance Survey maps (1964), reprinted from the 'Amateur Historian', National Council of Social Service.

Humphries, S. (1984) *Handbook for oral history: recording life stories*, Inter-Action Inprint.

Lance, David (1978) *An archive approach to oral history*, Imperial War Museum.

Linkman, Audrey (1991) *Caring for your family photographs at home*, Documentary Photography Archive.
Useful short introduction.

Lock, A. (1994) Living Memories of Hyde: using volunteers in an oral history project, *Local Studies Librarian*, **13** (2), 11-15.

Luft, N. (1991) *Preservation of the 'Northern Echo'*, Occasional paper No. 4, Department of Information and Library Management, Faculty of Art and Design, University of Northumbria at Newcastle.

MacDougall, J. (1994) *NEWSPLAN: guidelines for the microfilming of newspapers*, NEWSPLAN.

Makepeace, Chris (1985) *Ephemera: a book on its collection, conservation and use*, Gower.

Makepeace, C. (1996) Local history. In Lea, P. and Day, A. (eds) *The reference sources handbook*, 4th edn, Library Association Publishing, 144–83.

NEWSPLAN (1994) *Current perspectives on newspaper preservation and access: report of the 2nd National NEWSPLAN conference*, NEWSPLAN.

NEWSPLAN, millennia and grids: the digital challenges (1998), Information North.

Nichols, Harold (1976) *Map librarianship*, Clive Bingley.

Norrington Valerie (1989) *Recording the present: Local Historian at work 2*, BALH.

Oliver, Richard (1993) *Ordnance Survey maps: a concise guide for historians*, Charles Close Society.

Parry, David (1998) *Virtually new: creating the digital collection. A review of digitisation projects in local authority libraries and archives. A report to the Library and Information Commission by Information North*, Information North.

Petty, Mike (1985) *The albatross inheritance: local studies libraries*, MCB University Press.

Pols, R. (1992) *Dating old photographs*, FFHS.

Rempel, Siegfried (1987) *Care of photographs*, N. Lyons Books.
  American, but very useful on storage boxes, wallets, environment and handling.

Researcher's guide to British film and television collections (1993), 4th edn, British Universities Film and Video Council.

Rickards, Maurice (2000) *Encyclopaedia of ephemera: a guide to the fragmentary documents of everyday life for the collector, curator and historian*, British Library.

Sails, Pauline (1992) Yesterday's Yate: experimenting with oral history, *Local Studies Librarian*, **11** (2), 3-7.

Sutcliffe, G. (1995) *Slide collection management in libraries and information units*, Gower.

Thompson, Paul (2000) *Voice of the past*, 3rd edn, Oxford University Press.

Ward, A. (1990) *Manual of sound archive administration*, Gower.

Winterbotham, Diana (1989) The other side of the poster, or, how not to collect ephemera, *Local Studies Librarian*, **8** (1) 14-16.

B6   Collection management

Adams, Philip M. (1999) Library publishing on a shoestring, *Local Studies Librarian*, **18** (1), 10-12.

Baynes-Cope, A. D. (1982) *Caring for books and documents*, British Museum.
  Sections on the enemies of books and 'what to do'.

British Photographers Liaison Committee (1994) *ABC of UK photographic copyright*, British Photographers Liaison Committee.

British Standard (2000) BS 5454: *Standard for storage and exhibition of archival documents*, BSI.

Bromwich, David (1987) Parish packs: the Somerset approach, *Local Studies Librarian*, **6** (2), 15–16.

Bryant, Philip (1997) *Making the most of our libraries: the report of two studies on the retrospective conversion of library catalogues in the UK and the need for a national strategy*, Research and Innovation Centre.

Cabinet Office (2000) *E-government interoperability framework*, available at **www.govtalk.gov.uk/egif.home.html**.

Carpenter, L., Shaw, S. and Prescott, A. (1998) *Towards the digital library. British Library initiatives for access programme*, British Library.

Chapman, Ann, Kingsley, Nicholas and Dempsey, Lorcan (1999) *Full disclosure: releasing the value of library and archive collections*, UKOLN.

Copyright, Designs and Patents Act 1988: Elizabeth II Chapter 48, HMSO.

Cornish, G. P. (2001) *Copyright: interpreting the law for libraries and archives*, 3rd rev edn, Library Association Publishing.

Covert, Kay (2001) How the OCLC CORC is helping to weave libraries into the Web, *Online Information Review*, **25** (1) 41–6.

Crabb, Sue and Gordon, Ruth (2000) Dronfield's local history zone, *Local Studies Librarian*, **19** (1), 10–12.

Department of Education and Employment (1997), *Connecting the learning society*, available at **http://www.open.gov.uk/dfee/grid/index.htm**.

Falk, Howard (1999) View through the display window, *Electronic Library*, **17** (4) 263–7.

Feather, J. P. (1996) *Preservation and the management of library collections*, Library Association Publishing.

Flowers, Anna (1999) Local history publishing at Newcastle Libraries and Information Service, *Local Studies Librarian*, **18** (1), 7–9.

Great Britain. Parliament Statutory Instrument (1995) *The Duration of Copyright and Rights in Performance Regulations*, HMSO (SI 1995 No 3297).

Harris, Oliver (1996) United we stand – Croydon's multidisciplinary, historical database, *ITs News*, **33**, 17–21.

Klak, Janet (1997) Pretty pixels, *Local Studies Librarian*, **16** (2), 2–9.

Klijn, Edwin and de Lusenet, Yola (2000) *In the picture: preservation and digitisation of European photographic collections*, European Commission on Preservation and Access.

Laing, Ken and Mander, David (1999) Where history and technology meet, *Library Association Record*, **98** (8), 420–1.

Lander, John (2000) Digital preservation society, *Scottish Libraries*, **14** (2) issue 80, 14–15.

Lee, Stuart D. (2001) *Digital imaging: a practical handbook*, Library Association Publishing.

Library and Information Commission (1998) *Building the New Library Network: report to government*, Library and Information Commission, available at

www.lic.gov.uk/publications/policyreports/building/

Local Studies Librarian, **13** (1), Summer 1994.

Marchant, David and Hume, Eileen (1998) Visiting Knowsley's past, *Library Association Record*, **100** (9), 468–470.

Matthews, G. and Eden P. (1996) *Disaster management in British libraries: project report with guidelines for library managers*, British Library.

Maxted, Ian (1997) What's new, what's cool? Surf Devon and see, *Local Studies Librarian*, **16** (1), 10-11.

National Preservation Office (1998) *If disaster strikes!*, NPO.

New Library: the people's network (1997), Library and Information Commission for Department of Culture, Media and Sport. Published as a command paper CM 3887, 1998, available at **www.ukoln.ac.uk/services/lic/newlibrary/full.html**

New Opportunities Fund (2001) *nof-digitise Technical Standards and Guidelines*, available at **www.peoplesnetwork.gov.uk/nof/technicalstandards.html**

Nicholson, C. (1998) Locate GUI around the edges, *Local Studies Librarian*, **17** (2), 2-5.

Norman, Sandy (1999) *Copyright in public libraries*, 4th edn, Library Association Publishing.

Ostrow, Stephen (1998) *Digitizing historical pictorial collections for the internet*, Council on Library and Information Resources, Washington DC.

Ovenden, Richard (1999/2000) The baby and the bath water: sales of books and manuscripts, *Rare Books Newsletter*, 62-63 (Summer 1999–Winter 1999/2000) 24-49.

Contains Rare Books Group guidelines with commentary.

Parry, David (1998) *Virtually new. Creating the digital collection. A review of digitisation projects in local authority libraries and archives. A report to the Library and Information Commission by Information North*, Information North.

Pedley, P. (2000) *Copyright for library and information professionals*, 2nd edn, Aslib.

Phillips, Andrew (ed.) (2000) *The people's heritage: a new partnership for a national resource*, British Library.

Post, J. B. and Foster, M. R. (1992) *Copyright: a handbook for archivists*, Society of Archivists.

Scarborough, Michael (1997) Yorkshire Television Video History Project, *Local Studies Librarian*, **16** (2), 13-15.

Society of Archivists (1994) *Best practice guideline No 2: Security*, Society of Archivists.

Society of Archivists (1996) *Best practice guideline No 3: Health and safety: a guide to good health and safety practice in the record office*, Society of Archivists.

Society of Archivists. Preservation and Conservation Group (1994) *Directory of suppliers: a comprehensive list of suppliers and services for all preservation and conservation needs in archives, museums and libraries*, Society of Archivists.

Society of Archivists, Scottish Region (1996) *Disaster preparedness: guidelines for archives and libraries*, Society of Archivists, Scottish Region.

Tregarthen-Jenkin, I. (1987) *Disaster planning and preparedness: an outline disaster control plan*, British Library.

Wall, R. A. (1998) *Copyright made easier*, 2nd edn, Aslib.

Ward, A. (1994) *Copyright, ethics and oral history*, Oral History Society.

Watson, Iain (1996) The Durham Record, *Local Studies Librarian*, **15** (2), 2-6.

B7   Staff

Library Association (2000) *The use of volunteers in public libraries*, The Library Association.

B8   Facilities management

British Standards Institution (BS5454:2000) *Recommendations for the storage and exhibition of archival documents.*

Kitching, Christopher (1993) *Archive buildings in the United Kingdom 1977-1992*, Royal Commission on Historical Manuscripts.

Useful sections on storage, security and conversion of existing buildings.

Martin, Don (1994) Local studies at the new Kirkintilloch library, *Local Studies Librarian*, **13** (2), 2-4.

Index

accommodation 53-4
aims 1-2
Annual Library Plan 3-4
archaeologists 10
archival stationery 55
archives 33-4
archivists 12, 22-3, 24

benchmarking 3
Best Value 2-3
book publication *see* publishing
bookstock 25-7
branch libraries 14-15, 38

CD-ROM *see* ICT
cataloguing 40-5
charging for services 45
classification 40
collection policy 24-5
commercial users 10-11
community groups 16, 51-2
community libraries *see* branch
   libraries
conditions of use 36
conservation 35-8
   conservation materials 55
copyright 29, 30, 48
customers 1, 6-11

digitization *see* ICT
disabled people 10
disaster plans 37-8
discards 39
disposal of stock 39
donations 25, 38-9
drawings 32
duplicate material 39, 54

economic historians 9
educational publishing 47-8
engravings 32
enquiries 7
   measurement of 2, 3, 22
environment (storage) 36
ephemera 28
   cataloguing 40
equipment 53-8

ethnic groups 10, 18
events 20
exhibitions 19-20

family historians 9
films 32-3
   film archives 13
folklorists 9
friends groups 51-2
funding 5, 24-5, 44
furniture 53-4
future users 11, 17

geographers 9-10
geologists 9-10
grant aid 5

ICT
   cataloguing 40-5
   CD-ROMs 33, 47, 58
   digitization 30, 32, 41-5, 56
   disaster plan 37
   electronic publishing 47
   equipment 57-8
   networking 42-4
   planning 4-5
   promotion via the internet 21
   virtual resources 33
   websites 21
illustrations 29-32
   digitization 42-3
income generation 45-8
indexing 40-5
internet *see* ICT

lecturers 3, 8
lending collections 26-7
librarian 49-50
libraries (non local studies)
   13-15
lifelong learning 4
lighting 53
local authority publications 26
local government officers 15
local historians 8
local history groups 16
local studies

definition 1
local studies centres 22-3
maps 28-9, 37
   digitization 42
marketing 17-23
   of publications 46
media 15-16
   interviews 21
metadata 44-5
microform 27, 36
microform readers 55-6
moving images 32-3
   see also film archives
museums 12-13, 22-4

negatives 30, 37
news cuttings 28
newsletters 28
newspapers 27-8
   online 44
   relations with newspaper staff
      16, 20-1
NEWSPLAN 27

objectives 1-2
office accommodation 54
open access provision 54-5
Ordnance Survey 29
   digitization 42

People's Network 4, 43-4
performance indicators 2-4, 22
periodicals 27-8
photocopiers 56
photocopying 36
photographs 29-32
   copying 45
   digitization 42-3
   photographic equipment 56
planning 3-4
plans 28-9
postcard publishing 47
postcards 30
press releases 20-1
prints 32
promotion 15-23
   monitoring of 2

public areas 53
publications 18, 20, 46-8
publishing 18, 20, 46-8

radio 15-16
regulations 36
repairs 36, 55
reproduction rights 45, 48
    see also photocopying,
        photograph copying
right of access 48

schoolchildren 8, 13
security 35, 53-4
selection 25-6
shelving 54

slides 31
social audit 17
social historians 9
social inclusion 6-7, 17, 18
sound archives 13
sound recordings 32-3
    equipment 57
staff 49-52
standards 2-4
stock
    collection 24-34
    collection policy 24-5
    management 38-40
storage 36, 53-4
    equipment 55
students 8

talks 19
targets 2-4
teachers 8,13
television 15 -16
tourists 11
training 50-51
transport historians 9

users 1, 6-11

video 33
    equipment 57
volunteers 51-2

watercolours 32